Good Policy, Good Practice

Series Editors: Kirsti Nilsen and Martin Dowding

1. *Library Collection Development Policies: Academic, Public, and Special Libraries*, by Frank Hoffmann and Richard Wood. 2004.
2. *Library Collection Development Policies: School Libraries*, by Frank W. Hoffmann and Richard J. Wood. 2004.

Library Collection Development Policies

School Libraries and Learning Resource Centers

Frank W. Hoffmann
Richard J. Wood

Good Policy, Good Practice, No. 2

The Scarecrow Press, Inc.
Lanham, Maryland • Toronto • Plymouth, UK
2007

SCARECROW PRESS, INC.

Published in the United States of America
by Scarecrow Press, Inc.
A wholly owned subsidary of
The Rowman & Littlefield Publishing Group, Inc.
4501 Forbes Boulevard, Suite 200, Lanham, Maryland 20706
www.scarecrowpress.com

Estover Road
Plymouth PL6 7PY
United Kingdom

British Library Cataloguing in Publication Information Available

Library of Congress Cataloging-in-Publication Data

Hoffmann, Frank W., 1949–
    Library collection development policies : school libraries and learning resource
centers / Frank W. Hoffmann, Richard J. Wood.
        p. cm. — (Good policy, good practice ; no. 2)
    Includes bibliographical references and index.
    ISBN-13: 978-0-8108-5181-8 (pbk. : alk. paper)
    ISBN-10: 0-8108-5181-4 (pbk. : alk. paper)
  1. Collection development (Libraries)—United States. 2. Collection development
(Libraries)—United States—Policy statements. I. Wood, Richard J. (Richard John) II.
Title.

Z687.2.U6H65 2007
025.2'1—dc22   2007003009

Contents

Preface

This work—along with the companion volume devoted to academic, public, and special library collection development policies—represents an outgrowth of our *Library Collection Development Policies: A Reference and Writers' Handbook*, published by Scarecrow Press in 1996, which attempted to (1) ascertain why a well-organized policy makes good sense, (2) outline the strategies behind the creation and implementation of such policies, (3) examine the key elements comprising such documents, and (4) provide useful models culled from a wide range of library settings. These updated sourcebooks will focus on the latter two concerns in even greater detail, dissecting policies part by part and incorporating exemplary components from existing library manuals.

While collection development policies remain as vital to the integrity of library collection building as ever, the process also warrants reexamination in light of the many changes occurring in the information industry, libraries, library consortia, and educational institutions since the mid-1990s. The professional literature, our own experiences within the library world, and feedback from others in the field underscored that those changes, and their impact on library collection development policy, had been significant.

Not too many decades ago, collection development librarians only had to consider monographs and print journal subscriptions for the vast majority of their acquisitions. Matters remained relatively simple even as the imperatives for selecting and acquiring new audio, video, and micromedia formats increased. Nearly all selection and acquisition processes were handled using paper forms until the 1990s in most libraries. Some of these audio, video, and micromedia formats have come and gone over the decades, but books, documents, and serials are now available in both print and electronic formats.

Regarding audio resources, we considered that the compact disc (typically known as CD) became the preferred format in libraries for music by the early 1990s, but had not made equal gains within the reference field. By that time, the vast majority of librarians, in fact, seemed to be leery of the CD-ROM format for reference tools because hardware, software, archival, and other issues had not been resolved. Compact discs themselves were inexpensive, but they required the use of computer hardware and software that in turn necessitated ongoing maintenance and upgrading, as well as annual license renewal in many cases. The picture has been further complicated by the rise of various forms of enhanced CDs, the closely related DVD medium (and its competing high-definition spin-offs, Blu-ray and HD DVD), and various electronic forms of storage available via online or wireless transmission.

Monographs, audio, visual and some nonsubscription electronic resources can be purchased not only traditionally (directly from publishers and indirectly through jobbers), but also electronically through the Internet. Libraries may acquire books from jobbers who accept traditional paper orders or electronic ordering systems that allow selectors to build and transmit electronic book carts. Collection development policies should certainly address these developments.

These types of ordering processes do not apply to subscribed electronic resources because signed license agreements must be negotiated and signed by authorized agents of the respective companies and libraries or library networks. The means by which electronic media are acquired or licensed has become a complex issue often requiring the combined attention of collection developers, users, curriculum and technology coordinators closely associated with librarians, lawyers, and support agencies such as regional education service centers. Let us examine a few cases in point, which—though generally first addressed by academic, public, and special libraries—are having an increased impact on school settings.

Books are not available only in the traditional paper configuration, but also in nonprint or digitized formats such as CD-ROM. Digitized books may also be downloaded through the Internet by library users based on the terms of license agreements. Internet-accessible electronic text services have revolutionized how information is accessed by anyone with a networked personal computer. The vast majority of information seekers today look to the Internet, not libraries, as their initial data source, whether it is a company's webpage, a university's catalog, a virtual tour of a museum, a telephone directory, or a commercial database. Nearly every library and household these days uses the Internet to access information about nearly any topic anywhere in the world. When we wrote the *Writers' Handbook* in 1995, very few library policies were available electronically, and few librarians used e-mail and listservs.

Now librarians can employ the Internet to access collection development policies representing thousands of libraries, find their e-mail addresses, and write them with questions or comments about their policies. These approaches have the potential for bypassing the library altogether, as well as significantly impacting library collection development policy.

As the most revolutionary change since the invention of the printing press centuries earlier, the Internet is ushering out the use of CD-ROM reference tools and books in libraries. As far back as 2002, Questia had digitized more than sixty thousand electronic books, which are available to students or other users for a modest monthly fee paid either by the individual or an institution (calibrated as a per-student fee). Some larger and better-funded libraries or library systems have found it advantageous to license Questia, though most libraries feel it is the responsibility of their clientele to pay Questia's monthly rates. Another innovative company, ebrary, began selling digitized content by the page at the same time. Websites such as Internet Archive have proven even more liberating in providing hundreds of thousands of book, audio, and video resources by 2006 to the casual user legally and free of charge.

The Internet is now the preferred way to access journal articles from remote databases produced by library industry giants such as EBSCO, InfoTrac, Elsevier, Wiley, and LexisNexis. These full-text journal article databases are licensed to individual libraries, library systems, and groups of libraries (consortia) at a premium (percentage) above the cost of their print subscriptions. The premiums for electronic access set by these companies vary widely, as do their annual increases and pricing models. With respect to collection development policy, it is nearly impossible to develop anything other than a very general approach to dealing with this unpredictability.

Multiyear networking agreements are nonetheless often preferred by vendors and libraries alike to contain their respective costs and, for member libraries, to increase the number of accessible titles. A network library can often gain access to all the titles held in common by the members and increase the total number of accessible titles by canceling duplicates in addition to adding unique titles for an overall increase in the number of accessible titles. The cost of such licenses, however, has tended to increase nearly as much as the underlying journals. So libraries have tended to pay for the licenses by canceling print subscriptions where feasible. The feasibility of canceling print subscriptions when licensing full-text equivalent titles, however, means different things to different librarians. Ideally, most librarians could agree that it is easier to cancel a print subscription that is common to several vendors such as EBSCO, ProQuest, and Gale, but harder for titles that are unique to a single vendor such as Elsevier, which has a history of higher-than-average journal price increases. The problem for those libraries that cancel print subscriptions in order to pay for such licenses will come when there are insufficient funds to continue the licenses and the libraries end up with fewer print subscriptions while losing electronic access to hundreds of others.

An additional problem may be the archival policies (or lack thereof) of the companies that license such full-text article databases and their impact on collection development policy. Many libraries that have acquired JSTOR databases, for instance, have confidently withdrawn print backruns to save space because they trust the archival practices of JSTOR and the fact that research libraries are preserving print copies to ensure permanent availability. Many of the previously noted vendors do not inspire the confidence of librarians and users in that they are motivated by, and depend upon, making profits to stay in business.

While these companies chiefly make journal literature available to end users through libraries by means of license agreements, they may also provide articles and electronic books directly to end users in the home or office. In addition, scholars, writers, or other individuals with Internet-accessible computers may make their own publications available, free of charge, to the end user. Since the 1990s, scholars, academicians, doctors, government agencies, businesses, and others have been posting reports and drafts of their publications on their websites at an increasing rate. The Internet, therefore, has room for individuals, companies, government agencies, and jobbers to make the entire array of scholarly and nonscholarly literature available to anyone who has access to a networked personal computer. As a result, an increasing percentage of the world's literature is accessible from nonsubscribed journals or databases, outside of libraries. This trend is bound to influence scholarly communication as well as library collection development policy.

All of these issues have come to the forefront since the *Writers' Handbook* was published. We do not recall examining many library collection development policies in 1994 that included selection criteria and policies addressing either CD-ROM databases or electronic access to remote information databases. Few library collection development policies in the *Writers' Handbook*, in fact, addressed the selection, archiving, accessing, or licensing of electronic resources. Internet search engines, company websites, and library home pages as we know them today were not in use at that time. Like the policies of other large university and research libraries, California State University's policy—included in the *Writers' Handbook* (pp. 79–142)—recognized the development of end-user electronic services and resources. The CSU policy statement included a section on network-based materials (pp. 99–100) and envisioned the widespread, nearly ubiquitous, use of the full-text article databases now common in libraries of all sizes and types. CSU's policy also referred to the use of HyperCards, multimedia, CD-ROM towers, or multiple disc drives that were not yet prevalent in smaller academic, public, and school libraries. Tarlton Law Library's policy statement in the *Writers' Handbook* (p. 405) not only acknowledged CD-ROMs from West and other publishers as a growing component of its collection, but also noted the disadvantages of the format. Furthermore, Tarlton's policy acknowledged "difficult searching software, the need to change disks, the inability to down-load searches, etc., are reasons to decide against electronic formats even where the access and price criteria have been met." Mediated database searches by librarians were still the norm in the early 1990s even in the largest academic libraries, so few library policy statements addressed selection criteria for electronic databases or license agreements.

Since 1995, the aforementioned vendors have been developing their full-text digitized article databases and search engines for Internet access. An added impetus for these companies has been the rapidly expanding distance education programs. These advances are noteworthy because they have affected how users want to retrieve information as well as how libraries provide it. The licensing of full-text article databases from such companies has altered how libraries provide access to the journal literature and how users look for information. The now-common practice of licensing electronic resources on an annual basis in academic, public, special, and school libraries has altered reference, interlibrary loan, collection development, collection assessment, and other programs. Providing electronic databases has also altered how users retrieve, disseminate, and think about information.

As a result of these changes, we concluded that new policy examples would be needed to illustrate best practices. Both the volume concerned with academic, public, and special libraries and the one focusing on school libraries could be employed to illustrate how collection development policies have been significantly impacted by these comparatively recent technological advances.

The development of the "virtual library" has, in a word, caused many libraries to develop their first policy statements—or to update their existing documents—to account for the advances noted above. Whether the impetus for writing or revising is concern about illegal electronic access, filtering, privacy, copyright, plagiarism, archiving, preservation, or other issues, it remains a good idea for libraries to possess comprehensive collection development policies. In fact, censors have been a leading reason for librarians to look to their collection development policies for defense against using filtering software.

A basic and perplexing issue is whether or not these practices will continue for an extended period of time. At present, there is so much variability and instability in the information industry that few librarians are likely to count on the permanency of any license, not to mention technical and archival issues that complicate the entire environment. Users want free and easy access, libraries want value at a reasonable price, and vendors want to recover their initial costs and realize some degree of profit. It is in the best interests of all parties to work toward a stable and sustainable arrangement that is mutually beneficial.

Another motivation for reorganizing the format employed in the *Writers' Handbook* is the fact that many library collection development policies are accessible through the Internet via simple Web search strategies. Readers who wish to see a given document in its entirety can find the library's policy on the Internet, either by using the accompanying Web address supplied at the end of each excerpt or simply searching with keywords such as "collection development policy" and the institution name. Many librarians have developed written policies by reworking models (many of which have been posted on the Internet by state government agencies or library consortiums) to fit the imperatives of their own particular institutions. However, we believe that the close-up lens approach of providing background information devoted to the various policy components, complemented by representative excerpts from existing library documents, will spur greater facility in upgrading collection development policies as well as composing them in complete form.

Acknowledgments

We would like to thank those school libraries that permitted the reproduction of portions of their collection development policies within this book. A complete institutional list can be found in Appendix A.

We also appreciate the willingness of the American Library Association to permit reproduction of many of its intellectual freedom policy statements in Appendix B. Many additional related statements can be found at the ALA's official website, www.ala.org.

In addition, we would like to acknowledge the ongoing care and support provided by both of our wives, Lee Ann Hoffmann and Lynne Wood. They have been very understanding about the huge investment of time required to carry out this project.

Introduction

This work represents an ongoing effort to fill the void in the library literature relating to collection development policies. Our experience spans four decades as library educators and practitioners, and we created this book—as well as the earlier volume devoted to academic, public, and special libraries—to assist both library school students and professionals in the field with the compilation, revision, and implementation of policies. Given the premise that a well-rounded policy reflects all activities concerning the collection management process—including the evaluation, selection, acquisition, and weeding of information resources—we hope that the work will also prove useful to nonlibrarians possessing some kind of stake in high-quality library holdings. This intended audience might include school board members, local politicians, administrators, professional educators working closely with librarians, and taxpayers (including parents of students).

Considering the diversity of libraries by size, type, and service philosophy, it follows that the architecture of collection development policies should vary considerably from one institution to another. Likewise, the character of school media center policies are influenced by many factors, including

1. whether the policy is concerned with a site or an entire district;
2. the governance of the institution(s) covered (most notably, whether support is public or private in nature);
3. the presence of any specialized educational agenda (e.g., denominational affiliation, magnet school program); and
4. clientele profile, including age range, level of achievement, and family demographics.

The mode of presentation characterizing a given policy is also determined by a number of factors, most notably the sections comprising the document; the arrangement of these sections; the style of writing; the degree of reliance upon outside guidelines, forms, procedures, and the like; and physical format employed (i.e., a traditional print layout as opposed to mounting on an institution's website, complete with hyperlinks to individual sections). As demonstrated by the examples provided under the respective policy component breakdowns comprising the bulk of this volume, even when libraries share a similar outlook regarding collection building, they are likely to differ as to how they organize information as well as in the actual language of the headings they employ.

The policy components represented here constitute standardized sections most likely to be found in school library collection development statements. After surveying literally hundreds of policies available for in-house library use, within monographs, or posted on the Internet, the authors feel safe in proposing that there is nothing approaching consensus regarding the structure of these documents. In Chapter 1 of *Library Collection Development Policies: A Reference and Writers' Handbook*, we discussed at length the advantages to libraries of formulating collection development statements. Despite the efforts of library schools, scholars, professional associations, and other organizations to spread the gospel regarding written policies, many libraries continue to carry out the vital function of collection management without any form of documented plan. The bewildering array of policies available to the beginning collection developer may be in part responsible for their absence in some libraries. The headings below—along with the introductory discussion and excerpted policies—represent an attempt to impart some sense of clarity and uniformity to this rather chaotic state of affairs.

The work is divided into three major sections: the first focuses on elements that enable these documents to serve as a blueprint for building library holdings; the next explores the ethical and legal issues ensuing from the use of digital resources; and the last addresses digital information within the context of traditional library operations. Appendix A identifies the school libraries providing material that serves either as model examples or to aptly illustrate the function of various policy statements. Addresses and phone numbers have been provided to enable the reader to contact these libraries for further information—most notably, complete or updated copies of their respective policies. In cases where the policy has been published on the Internet, Web addresses are included following the excerpted portion in the Selection Policy Components section. (In cases where the web addresses have been changed or no longer function properly, search the URL in the Wayback Machine, located at www.archive.org.) Appendix B includes the text of American Library

Association documents frequently included in collection development policies. The ALA has long advocated that libraries promulgate policies and apply them to the ongoing process of collection building. To this end, the ALA encourages libraries to incorporate these statements—and other information resources available from its website—into their respective policies. This segmented approach offers a more manageable guide to the rather daunting task of collection development policy formulation. Addressing sections that—taken as a whole—comprise a policy also serve as a realistic roadmap for executing updates on an incremental basis as needed.

Chapter One

Collection Development Policy Introduction

A substantial number of school library collection development policies begin with an introductory section, often without a heading, which can serve one or more of the following functions:

1. To provide a rationale for the policy as a whole
2. To delineate the uses of the document
3. To clarify terminology or concepts covered
4. To make a statement regarding the commitment of the library, school, or district to certain educational objectives
5. To identify the individuals and/or groups responsible for its formulation

In some policies, the introduction provides a smooth transition into the next portion of the document. For example, this section is appended by the library/media center objectives in the Wilmington School District policy included below. In other instances, it incorporates components—often without the benefit of subheadings—that typically stand alone. The Baltimore County Public Schools policy serves as a case in point, incorporating the "Responsibility for Collection Development" and "Gifts" statements within its second paragraph.

SAMPLE POLICIES

Baltimore County (Towson, Maryland) Public Schools

Selection Criteria for School Library Media Center Collections

The Baltimore County Public Schools policy states that each office in the Department of Instruction shall establish a Materials Review and Selection

Committee to determine criteria for selecting materials to ensure that all instructional materials extend the knowledge and understanding of the Essential Curriculum. The following policy was developed by the Office of Library
and Information Technology.

School library media specialists are responsible for the review, evaluation,
and selection of the school library media collection. They are guided by the sys-
tem-level selection policy that embodies the philosophy and procedures set
forth in national, state, and county documents. Library media specialists work
cooperatively with administrators and teachers to provide resources which represent diverse points of view, stimulate growth in thinking skills, and promote
the overall educational program. Library media collections are developed to
meet both curricular and personal needs. To ensure that these needs are met, library media specialists apply selection criteria and use recommended selection
tools. All purchases, including gifts, should meet the same selection standards.

This selection policy reflects the philosophy and goals of the school system and supports the principles of intellectual freedom described in *Information Power: Guidelines for School Library Media Programs*, the *Library Bill
of Rights* (American Library Association), *Students' Right to Read* (NCTE),
and other position statements on intellectual freedom [cited documents include hyperlinks] from ALA and the American Association of School Librarians. The Baltimore County Public Schools are in compliance with federal
laws regarding Internet safety and protection by requiring a filtering proxy
server on the district wide area network (see Baltimore County Public
Schools Telecommunications Policies and Rules). [www.bcps.org/offices/lis/
office/admin/selection.html]

School District of Philadelphia Library Programs and Services

Selection Policy for School Library Materials

Philosophy of the Library/Instructional Materials Center   We are living
in an information age. A primary objective of education is to learn how to
identify, locate, organize, and present needed information in a clear, concise,
and persuasive manner. As technologies change, students need to develop
skills to manage complex information formats. The school library program,
as an integral part of the total curriculum, is the vehicle that provides opportunities for students to achieve these skills and to foster a lifelong interest in
both reading and knowledge. Each student, therefore, should have access to
an effective, integrated school library program that reflects the curriculum
and the needs of the school community and the world in general. [adopted
November 15, 1996 by the Philadelphia Board of Education; revised February 5, 2002; www.libraries.phila.k12.pa.us/misc/selection-policy.html]

Squires Elementary School (Fayette County, Kentucky) Library

Collection Development & Materials Selection Policy

The collection development policy is meant to serve as a guide to the professional staff of the Squires Elementary School Library, and also as a source of information about policies and procedures of the library to others of the library community.

The word "materials" in this document applies to books, pamphlets, magazines, newspapers, microforms, recording, films, filmstrips, videocassettes, audiocassettes, compact discs, slides, transparencies, charts, posters, teaching sets, kits, pictures, media equipment, and computer software.

The Code of Ethics adopted by the American Library Association (June 30, 1981) is used as it applies to the duties of the school library media specialist (librarian). [www.squires.fcps.net/library/policies.htm]

Wilmington (Vermont) School District

Collection Development Policy

Introduction The collection development policy of the library/media centers within the Wilmington School District looks to each school's statement of purpose wherein are specified the goals to provide opportunities so that students may reason; think independently, critically and creatively; analyze problems and propose solutions; take responsibility; achieve personal excellence in academic skills; utilize current technology with competence; contribute to a school atmosphere conducive to learning; appreciate their community and its values; and value the role of diversity and tolerance in our society.

We recognize that to achieve these goals and the other goals of our philosophy, we must continue to provide free access to information, which is a hallmark of our democratic society. We also realize that new and developing technologies continue to have an impact on teaching and learning, especially increasing our ability to acquire information from a variety of sources. These new technologies demonstrate that we are a part of a global community, which is as close as we allow our technology to bring it.

The major expectations of the Wilmington Middle/Senior High School and the Deerfield Valley Elementary School library/media centers are that they will support the schools' curricula with print and nonprint materials, including reference materials, in-depth works, and current newspapers and journals. A wide range of materials at all appropriate levels of difficulty, with diversity of appeal, and with different points of view will be provided. Every effort will be made to obtain additional material from other sources (i.e., interlibrary loan). Within assigned curricula, students will be provided with instruction in research skills, including the ability to seek information using up-to-date technology.

The library/media centers' collections of print and nonprint materials and the technological resources they offer to faculty and students are vital to the implementation of Vermont's Framework of Standards and Learning Opportunities. The collection also provides the student with ample opportunities to apply and demonstrate information literacy skills as delineated in "Using Vermont's Common Core: Information Literacy for Vermont Students, A Planning Guide." (These documents are on file in the district media centers.)

Responsibility for development of this policy lies with the librarians and the technology coordinators. The principals, librarians, and technology coordinators will take part in the ongoing development process, as the policy is approved and revised. [www.dves.k12.vt.us/Users/cethier/libpol.html]

Chapter Two

Mission, Goals, and Objectives Statements

Although widely employed within written policies, this section poses a number of problems for anyone referring to these documents. In many instances, libraries don't utilize mission, goals, and objectives statements in tandem, despite the fact that these three concepts are interrelated and vital to the overall collection-building plan. This shortcoming may be a result of confusion in the way some libraries interpret these concepts. Elizabeth Futas has alluded to the lack of consistency from one library to another in the application of these terms, noting that policies "often called them mission statements when they were goals, goals when they were objectives, and objectives when they were goals."[1]

Some libraries opt for including mission, goals, and objectives statements that address the full spectrum of library services. In such cases, those statements specifically geared to collection development may be hard to discern or absent altogether. Furthermore, it is doubtful that many of the statements appearing in policies have been formulated based on sound data, so the likelihood of a library achieving published goals and objectives is questionable.

Given the widespread misuse of these terms, it would seem instructive to delineate their meaning and application. According to Futas, a mission statement "should be short, general, and long-lived," while complementing the mission of the parent institution, if there is one.[2] In order to fulfill the mission, goals should articulate library priorities in the form of broad, albeit focused, purpose statements. Typically beginning with words like "develop," "provide," "encourage," or "support," goals should be achievable within a ten-year period. Best seen as incremental steps that enable an institution to achieve its goals and mission, objectives should be measurable, specific, determinate, and action oriented.[3]

SAMPLE POLICIES

The contrast between general statements incorporating issues, which encompass more than collection management, and those focusing on collection building proper is reflected in the documents cited here. Furthermore, examples can be seen to vary considerably regarding the depth of coverage devoted to delineating this operation. The Apponequet Regional High School Library provides a broad-based approach spanning the full range of library services, with collection-building concerns emphasized at the "objectives" level. On the other hand, the Mt. Ararat High School Library and School District of Philadelphia focus exclusively on the role development of library holdings plays.

Apponequet Regional High School (Lakeville, Massachusetts) Library

Collection Development and Mission Statements

Mission   The Apponequet Regional High School Library was established to support the curriculum of the high school in which it is located.

All students, grades nine through twelve, are serviced. The library exists to implement, enrich, and support the educational program of the school.

It is the intent of the library to serve as the hub of intellectual activity at the school.

It is therefore the library's mission "to ensure that students and staff are effective users of ideas and information."

Goals

1. The library will serve the intellectual and educational needs of the school in varied ways: "by providing intellectual and physical access to materials in all formats"; "by providing instruction to foster competence and stimulate interest in reading, viewing, and using information and ideas"; through acquisition of and assistance with new technologies of service and instruction; and through provision of materials to incite and excite recreational reading.
2. The library will provide a facility to serve the intellectual and educational needs of the school through the provision and coordination of meeting areas, viewing areas, classroom and production areas.
3. It is a goal of the Apponequet Regional High School Library staff to provide an atmosphere conducive to learning, yet one which is comfortable, pleasing and relaxing.
4. It is a goal of the library to open its collection and facilities to the communities of Freetown and Lakeville as a whole, and to the staffs and stu-

dents of the George R. Austin Middle School, the Freetown Elementary School and Lakeville's Assawompset Elementary School.
5. It is a goal of the library to work "with other educators to design learning strategies to meet the needs of individual students."

Objectives In order to service the library's community of patrons and achieve the goals enumerated above, the following objectives are established for the Apponequet Regional High School Library:

1. The library will provide materials which will support the individual curricula of the school through a comprehensive selection process which involves library staff, students and teachers.
2. The library will provide materials which will support the educational enrichment needs of students: materials which will amplify and expand upon the curriculum which is offered and materials which go beyond the scope of the present educational curriculum.
3. The library will provide materials which offer remedial assistance to students. It will provide low-reading-level, high-interest-level materials which will spark interest amongst users of such materials.
4. The library will provide for career-oriented materials which will assist students in making career choices.
5. The library will provide materials for students seeking information on institutions of higher learning; it will provide material assistance for those seeking information on college applications, college essays, finances and scholarship availability.
6. The library will provide recreational reading interests of students through the provision of materials in fiction and nonfiction—for all students at all levels of reading development and shall include works which fall into many genres: classics as well as popular fiction.
7. The library will provide auxiliary materials which will assist teachers in the implementation of their curriculum, in conformity with objectives enumerated in *Information Power: Guidelines for School Library Media Programs*.
8. The library will provide intellectual access to information through systematic learning activities which develop cognitive strategies for selecting, retrieving, analyzing, evaluating, synthesizing, and creating information at all age levels and in all curriculum content areas.
9. The library will provide physical access to information through (a) a carefully selected and systematically organized collection of diverse learning resources, representing a wide range of subjects, levels of difficulty, communication formats, and technological delivery systems; (b) access to information and materials outside the library media center and the school

building through such mechanisms as interlibrary loan, networking and other cooperative agreements, and online searching of databases; and (c) providing instruction in the operation of equipment necessary to use the information in any format.

10. The library will provide learning experiences that encourage users to become discriminating consumer and skilled creators of information through introduction to the full range of communications media and the use of new and emerging information technologies such as distance learning and the Internet.

11. The library will provide leadership, instruction and consulting assistance in the use of instructional and information technology and the use of sound instructional design principles.

12. The library will provide resources and activities that contribute to lifelong learning, while accommodating a wide range of differences in teaching and learning styles and in instructional methods, interests, and capacities.

13. The library will provide a facility that functions as the information center of the school, as a locus for integrated, interdisciplinary, intergrade, and school-wide learning activities.

14. The library will provide resource and learning activities that represent a diversity of experiences, opinions, social and cultural perspectives, supporting the concept that intellectual freedom and access to information are prerequisite to effective and responsible citizenship in a democracy.

It is the responsibility of the school library media specialist to take the lead in translating the mission, goals, and objectives into programs that make effective access to information and ideas a reality.

However, achievement of this mission at the school level also requires

- full integration of the library media program into the curriculum;
- a partnership among the school library media specialist, district-level personnel, administrators, teachers and parents; and
- the serious commitment of each of those partners to the value of universal and unrestricted access to information and ideas.

[http://users.rcn.com/libra/mission.html]

Mt. Ararat High School (Topsham, Maine) Library

Materials Selection Policy

Objectives of Selection   The MSAD #75 Board of Directors recognizes that it is the primary objective of the library media centers in our schools to implement, enrich, and support the educational programs of the schools. It is the duty of the library media centers to provide a wide range of materials on all levels of difficulty, with diversity of appeal and the presentation of different points of view.

To this end, the Board of Education reaffirms the Bill of Rights for School Library Media Programs and asserts that the responsibility of the School Library Media Center is as follows:

1. To provide materials that will enrich and support the curriculum, taking into consideration the varied interests, abilities, and maturity levels of the students served
2. To provide materials that will stimulate growth in factual knowledge, literary appreciation, aesthetic values, and ethical standards
3. To provide a background of information which will enable students to make intelligent judgments in their daily life
4. To provide materials on opposing sides of controversial issues so that young citizens may develop under guidance the practice of critical of all media (Opinions expressed in library materials are not necessarily endorsed by the MSAD #75 Board of Education.)
5. To provide materials representative of the many religious, ethnic, and cultural groups and their contribution to our American heritage
6. To place principle above personal opinion and reason above prejudice in selection of materials of the highest quality in order to assure a comprehensive collection appropriate for the users of the library media center

In addition, the Board of Education recognizes that the final decision as to what materials an individual student will be exposed to rests with that student's parents or guardians. However, at no time will the wishes of one child's parents to restrict his/her reading or viewing of a particular item infringe on other parents' rights to permit their child to read or view the same material. [revised May 7, 1999; www.mta.link75.org/library/selection policy.html; www.mta.link75.org/library/index.html (then click on "Selection Policy" hyperlink)]

School District of Philadelphia Library Programs and Services

Selection Policy for School Library Materials

Selection Objectives   School library materials will be selected by the School District to support and enrich the educational program. Materials will serve both the breadth of the curriculum and the needs and interests of the faculty and students. It is the obligation of the District to provide for a wide range of abilities and to respect the diversity of many differing points of view as specified in Board Policy 102 (Multiracial-Multicultural-Gender Education).

Library materials are defined as all electronic, print, and nonprint resources, excluding textbooks, used by students and teachers for the District's educational program. [adopted November 15, 1996 by the Philadelphia Board of Education; revised February 5, 2002; www.libraries.phila.k12.pa.us/misc/selection-policy.html]

NOTES

1. Elizabeth Futas, ed., *Collection Development Policies and Procedures*, 3rd ed. (Phoenix, AZ: Oryx, 1995), 184–85.

2. Futas, *Collection Development Policies and Procedures*, 184.

3. Futas, *Collection Development Policies and Procedures*, 184.

Chapter Three

Responsibility for Collection Development

A fixture in most written policies, the "Responsibility" statement should clearly state the title of the individual ultimately responsible for collection building decisions. This responsibility is usually vested in one of the following administrative levels: the school site principal, the district superintendent, the school board, or some district-wide coordinator (heading up library services, technology, or curriculum development, among other divisions) with line authority over collection development. If any documents (e.g., applicable standards) beyond the policy itself help govern collection-building decisions, they are often cited in this section.

In many instances, the designated authority delegates responsibility to the staff involved with day-to-day selection decisions. In a setting including more than one trained library/media/information technology specialist, the department head or a staff member most qualified to oversee collection management activities will generally be assigned this role. The professional qualifications required of personnel in such a position should be noted in terminology easily understood by laypersons.

Some policies include a chart or figure outlining collection areas along with the staff member responsible for collection building within each category. As elsewhere, position titles should be employed rather than names of personnel because staff turnover often occurs more frequently than policy revisions.

Additional details relating to selection process are sometimes included, for example, the use of professional reviewing tools, consideration of purchase recommendations from library clientele (particularly site teachers, staff, students, and the community at large), and the like. Such information can prove useful in defusing outside criticism, particularly in cases of attempted censorship. If lengthy explanations are considered necessary, however, they probably should be included in their own sections.

SAMPLE POLICIES

The variety of approaches in responsibility statements generally reflects the differing governance of the respective school libraries. However, as the excerpts below make clear, libraries without exception advocate the administration of library affairs such as collection building by trained professionals.

Aldine Independent School District (Houston, Texas) Library Media Services Department

Policy and Procedures Manual

Responsibilities of the Library Media Specialist As stated in *Information Power: Building Partnerships for Learning*, library media specialists have always drawn upon a distinctive expertise about information, and a growing body of research is demonstrating the unique contribution this expertise can bring to student achievement. Especially in recent years, the profession has pioneered in identifying and meeting learning needs brought about by the rapid and continuing expansion of information delivered through a variety of new technologies. As an essential partner who both contributes to and draws from the expertise of the entire learning community, the library media specialist plays a role that

- begins with promoting and reinforcing students' interests and abilities in reading, listening, and viewing;
- expands to include fostering the full range of information concepts, strategies, and abilities that students must master to profit from the global resources that are quite literally at their fingertips; and
- includes developing the full range of abilities that students need to interact effectively with information and to construct meaningful knowledge.

To fulfill this role, the effective library media specialist draws upon a vision for the student-centered library media program that is based on collaboration, leadership, and technology. The library media specialist does this by acting as a teacher, an instructional partner, an information specialist, and a program administrator.

Relationships to other School Personnel: Principal Principals have a special role in developing and supporting the Library Media Center. The principal can evaluate the total interrelationship of the community and the school and is the library media specialist's most knowledgeable source of information and guidance.

Principals assist the Library Media Center by

- acting as a link to and from the district level;
- endorsing the Library Media Center program to teachers, students and parents;
- making school funds available whenever possible;
- observing the Library Media Center program, suggesting improvements, and supporting new programs; and
- keeping the library media specialist informed about curriculum changes.

The do's of a library specialist approaching a school administrator are as follows:

- Do make a scheduled appointment. Prepare to discuss issues.
- Do plan ahead. Make notes of points you want to emphasize.
- Do prepare a long-range plan of quantitative and qualitative goals for the year.
- Do take along statistics and research for support.
- Do prepare and submit a detailed request list for the library.
- Do emphasize the needs of the students and faculty members for media services.
- Do emphasize the importance of the paraprofessional doing clerical work so that you, as a professional, will be accessible to students and teachers.
- Do be considerate of the administrator's time, especially during the first two weeks of school.
- Do approach funding requests in a positive, timely, and enthusiastic manner.
- Do state your needs with the assurance that they are essential.
- Do see administrators two weeks after school begins.
- Do maintain a professional attitude at all times.

District Director of Library Media Services   The District Director of Library Media Services and Computer Services is a resource person for the campus library media staff and carries out responsibilities in the following areas:

- Consulting with administration on guidelines for the district Library Media Center program
- Developing and implementing business policies and procedures
- Helping to establish policy and set standards for the Library Media Services department
- Acting as a communication channel between the administration and school library media specialist

- Acting as a communication link between the Resource Center staff and library media specialists
- Interpreting district goals, objectives, procedures and budget to new schools
- Allocating local and federal funds for the purchase of Library Media Center basic collections for new schools
- Allocating local and federal funds for the purchase of Library Media Center books and audiovisual materials
- Overseeing the selection and organization of Library Media Center basic collections for new schools
- Planning and organizing for Library Media Center aides and teachers inservice training with the help of specialists and aides
- Informing specialists and principals of professional growth conferences, workshops, etc., and encouraging their attendance
- Observing the Library Media Centers and consulting with specialists and/or principals on improving the program and facilities
- Recommending materials and equipment to other district personnel
- Providing resources for district curriculum writers as requested
- Orienting new library media personnel
- Consulting with library media specialists regarding any special problems.
- Arranging and conducting bi-monthly meetings for library media specialists
- Acting as a link to the community, regional, and state level resources including public library systems and academic libraries, regional service centers, etc.
- Preparing necessary business forms and compiling records on the district level
- Preparing reports as requested by administrative personnel

Library Management Systems Administrator   The Library Management Systems Administrator has the following responsibilities:

- Oversees the operation and use of the library automation system and defines fiscal needs to ensure that resources address the mission of Aldine ISD
- Provides training on technology hardware and software as applicable to the library automation systems, as well as expanding technological developments
- Coordinates and is responsible for the pre-installation of automation systems at new campuses
- Serves as system administrator for the library automation in all school Library Media Centers and provides opportunities for staff development regarding network software

- Serves as liaison between school districts, companies, vendors, organizations and district personnel
- Analyzes facility and equipment needs for optimum use of the library automation system; utilizes information to make recommended changes or adjustments
- Supervises and assists with the automated cataloging of instructional materials in order to provide the best access of these materials to students and teachers
- Participates in the creation of a bibliographic and local authority database that is accurate, complete, and which will provide ready access to management
- Performs original cataloging of print and nonprint materials as directed by the Director of Library Media Services according to national standards (AACR2, Dewey Decimal System, Library of Congress Subject Headings, MARC formatting) for use in the district-wide catalog databases
- Coordinates the retrospective conversion of existing bibliographic records to MARC format for the district-wide catalog database of all library holdings.
- Supervises the maintenance of the district-wide database, thereby maintaining data integrity
- Develops and implements policies and procedures for works of original cataloging
- Serves as a resource person to library media specialists on automation, cataloging, and technical trends, and development affecting the library program

[revised June 1999; www.Aldine.k12.tx.us]

Bowling Green (Ohio) City School District

Media Center Materials Selection Policy

Selection Personnel   The Bowling Green City Board of Education is the legal body in which rests the ultimate responsibility for the selection of materials for the Bowling Green City Schools Media Centers. The responsibility for the actual selection of materials for the school media center shall be delegated to the professional librarian of each school based on the goals of the school system and the curriculum.

The personnel who assist in the actual selection of materials for the media centers must include the professional librarians, and may include other media specialists, curriculum consultants, teaching staff, administrators, other staff, students and parents. [last revised October 2002; http://winslo.state.oh.us/publib/material-bg.html; http://winslo.state.oh.us/publib/policies.html (then click on "Materials Selection" hyperlink)]

Chico (California) Unified School District

School Library Media Centers District Plan

Responsibility for Selection   The Board of Trustees is responsible for all materials in the library information centers of CUSD. The responsibility for selection of the materials is delegated to certified library media teachers. The library media teachers coordinate, select, and purchase all materials. While extensive advice is sought from administrators, teachers, specialists, teaching assistants, students, parents and others affiliated with the CUSD, final decisions for the selection of all materials lies with certified library media teachers. [published December 9, 1998; http://panther.chs.chico.k12.ca.us/libr/Plan/libplan.html]

Delaware Valley School District (Milford, Pennsylvania)

Library Collection Policy

Responsibility   The superintendent or designee will direct establishment of criteria to be followed by the Delaware Valley School District librarians under the direction of the building administrators. [adopted March 19, 1987; http://dvasdweb.dvasd.k12.pa.us/]

Groton (Connecticut) Public Schools Media Technology Services

Policies & Procedures

Responsibility

1. The Groton Board of Education assumes legal responsibility for the selection of materials in the district's library information centers.
2. Responsibility for the selection of all library materials is delegated to the professional library staff through the building principal. The selection process involves open opportunity for consultation with administrators, faculty, supervisors, and students. Selection is based upon evaluation by the professional library staff, using professional library tools and other review media.
3. In selecting materials, library, staff, administrators, and faculty are guided by the principles incorporated in the School Library Bill of Rights, the Freedom to Read Statement, standards adopted by the American Association of School Librarians, and the School Library Standards of the Connecticut State Department of Education.

4. The collection will be developed systematically, ensuring a well-balanced coverage of subjects, opinions, and formats and a wide range of materials on various levels of difficulty supporting the diverse interests, needs, and viewpoints of the school community.

[last updated: March 8, 1999; www.groton.k12.ct.us/mts/matselect.htm]

Chapter Four

Evaluative Criteria

This section, sometimes referred to as Selection Criteria, represents the core of the collection development policy. It provides a blueprint as to why certain information resources are chosen over others for library holdings. Therefore, listing criteria employed by collection developers informs an institution's constituency regarding the title-by-title decision-making process and expenditure of funds.

Policies vary to a considerable degree in the presentation of this information. Most notably, libraries do not always clearly differentiate between general and specific criteria, choosing instead to provide an inventory of points for consideration during the evaluation process. Libraries offering a more segmented layout may have contrasting perceptions of exactly what constitutes "general" criteria. Some institutions equate them with collection-building *objectives* (see the "Objectives" sections below for the Atwater Elementary School District and Rogers High School), that is, a mechanism for outlining the *purpose* of the overall process. Other libraries apply them as a device that facilitates viewing holdings as a single entity, whereas specific criteria are applied on a title-by-title basis. In other words, such general criteria serve as a corrective mechanism to ensure that collections remain focused on primary institutional goals and objectives. Typical examples of these general criteria would include the following:

- The collection will attempt to provide a balance of viewpoints on all controversial issues.
- The collection will attempt to include a cross-section of media formats, topics, and viewpoints representative of patron needs and interests.
- The library will attempt to meet all relevant collection standards, whether issued by governmental agencies, professional associations, or regional accrediting bodies.

Many libraries simply view general criteria as possessing the broadest possible application, whereas specific criteria are employed with particular media, categories, and so on, and separate as such. Specific criteria may also be organized by age level, subject area, and special collections.[1] In some cases, libraries incorporate both concepts into one all-inclusive listing. The Scecina Memorial High School policy reflects this approach.

Collection policies can include additional irregularities worthy of note. Evaluative criteria are occasionally found in other portions of the document, for example, the format statement, gifts, and weeding guidelines. In other instances, the library will apply the same set of criteria for both the selection and weeding functions. Elizabeth Futas provides justification for such a strategy: "What differs, after all, is the community for which it was selected versus the community for which it will be rejected, and the time it was selected versus the time it will be discarded. The process and the criteria remain the same."[2]

SAMPLE POLICIES

The varied approached noted above—use of general versus specific criteria, the integrated presentation of criteria, and so on—are reflected in the following policy examples.

Atwater (California) Elementary School District

Selection Policy for Books and Materials

Objectives   The school library/instructional media centers function to implement, enrich, and supplement the instructional program of the school as well as to provide for the independent study and personal reading of the students. In order to ensure that the school media program is an integral part of the educational program of the schools, the following selection objectives are supported:

- Learning resources, including textbooks, will support and be consistent with the general educational goals of the state and district, and the aims and objectives of individual schools and specific courses.
- Learning resources will meet high standards of quality in factual content and presentation.
- Learning resources will be designed to help students gain an awareness of our pluralistic society.

- Learning resources will be selected for their strengths rather than rejected for their weaknesses.

Criteria   Criteria for selection of textbooks will follow district textbook adoption policy.

In developing the library media collection, consideration should be given to the educational goals of the district, individual student learning modes, teaching styles, curricular needs, faculty and student needs, existing materials, and networking arrangements. The following points should be taken into account in the purchase of materials:

- Overall purpose
- Timeliness or permanence
- Importance of subject matter in relation to the curriculum
- Overall quality
- Integrity
- Favorable reviews found in standard selection sources
- High degree of potential user appeal
- Reputation of author, publisher, or producer
- Quality and variety of format
- Value commensurate with cost and/or need

Specific Criteria   Specific areas which have frequently been subject to criticism will be handled in the following ways:

1. Sex Instruction: Materials will be selected on the basis of sound factual authority considering the practical need for information of the young people who use the material.
2. Religion: Representative materials will be available for students studying comparative religions. An attempt will be made to provide factual, unbiased materials representative of all major religions.
3. Ideologies: Information and/or literary treatment on the philosophies of any group and all points of view on the issues of our times shall be represented according to the interests of our curriculum. Such information will be selected on the basis of its sound factual authority and/or literary merit.
4. Obscenity in materials of literary value: The use of profanity or sexual incidents shall not in itself disqualify material from selection. Decision to include such materials shall rest entirely upon stern tests of literary merit, whether the material presents life in its true proportions, in an artistic way, and in a manner which would allow the individual to form sound, ethical judgments.

5. Science: Material shall be selected according to its unbiased, objective and authoritative treatment of fact or theory. It will not be considered in relation to apparent agreement or conflict with moral or ethical judgments of ideological groups.
6. Discrimination: Materials will portray sexual, racial, religious, ethnic, or other social groupings in our society in such a way as to build positive images while supplying an accurate and sound balance in the matter of historical perspective.

[adopted 1990; http://mse.aesd.k12.ca.us/library/selectpol.html; www.aesd.edu/mse//library/libraries.html (then click on "Policies and Procedures" hyperlink)]

Rogers (Arkansas) Public School System

District Instructional Materials Selection Policy

Objectives of Selection   The primary objective of instructional materials is to implement, enrich, and support the educational program of the school. It is the duty of the schools to provide a wide range of materials on all levels of difficulty, with diversity of appeal, and presentation of different points of view.

To this end, the Board of Education of the Rogers Public School System adopts the statement of philosophy expressed by the American Association of School Librarians and the Association for Better Communication and Technology. The American Association of School Librarians reaffirms its belief in the Library Bill of Rights of the American Library Association. Media Specialists are concerned with generating understanding of American freedoms through the development of informed and responsible citizens. To this end, the American Association of School Librarians asserts that the responsibility of the school library media center is as follows:

1. Books and other library resources should be provided for the interest, information, and enlightenment of all people of the community the library serves. Materials should not be excluded because of the origin, background, or views of those contributing to their creation.
2. Libraries should provide materials and information presenting all points of view on current and historical issues. Materials should not be proscribed or removed because of partisan and doctrinal disapproval.
3. Libraries should challenge censorship in the fulfillment of their responsibility to provide information and enlightenment.

4. Libraries should cooperate with all persons and groups concerned with re-sisting abridgment of free expression and free access to ideas.
5. A person's right to use a library should to not be denied or abridged be-cause of origin, age, background, or views.
6. Libraries which make exhibit spaces and meeting rooms available to the public they serve should make such facilities available on an equitable ba-sis, regardless of the beliefs or affiliations of individuals or groups re-questing their use.

Criteria for Selection of Instructional Materials   Needs of the individual school are based on the following:

A. Requests of faculty and students
B. Knowledge and support of curriculum
C. Consideration the existing collection

Materials for purchase are considered on the basis of the following criteria:

A. Overall purpose
B. Timeliness or permanence
C. Importance of subject matter
D. Quality of writing/production/binding
E. Readability
F. Popular appeal
G. Accuracy
H. Reputation of publisher/producer
I. Reputation and significance of the author/composer/producer, etc.
J. Fformat and price

[www.rogers.k12.ar.us/users/mcook/selection.html (various specialized poli-cies can be reached by hyperlink, e.g., SBP-IJJ.PDF)]

Scecina Memorial High School (Indianapolis, Indiana)

Collection Development Policy

Criteria for Collection Development   The major criterion for the selection of resources is the educational suitability of the resource for its intended use. Me-dia specialists use educational criteria and professional judgment rather than per-sonal opinions, values, or beliefs in the selection of resources. All materials pur-chased or accepted as gifts for use in the Scecina Media Center will be evaluated according to the following criteria. Specific criteria are used as they apply:

1. Resources are consistent with the educational goals of Scecina and the goals and objectives of specific courses.
2. Resources are appropriate for the age, interests, abilities, learning styles, social development, and maturity levels of the students.
3. Resources provide information which will motivate students and staff to examine their own attitudes and behavior, to comprehend their duties, responsibilities, rights and privileges as participating citizens in our society, and to make informed judgments in their daily lives.
4. Resources represent the diversity of religious, ethnic, political and cultural values held in a pluralistic society.
5. Resources illustrate the contributions to our national heritage and the world made by various groups in our society.
6. Resources illustrate historical and contemporary forces in society to enable users to recognize and understand social, economic, and personal problems.
7. Resources provide a variety of points of view about issues, including those considered by some to be controversial.
8. Resources are selected for all student ability levels.
9. Resources are judged as a whole.
10. Resources meet standards of technical quality and physical condition appropriate to the format and their intended use.
11. Resources are judged according to the scope, arrangement and organization, relevance of information, special features, and overall value to the collection.

Selection of materials will be made on the merits of the material and its value to the collection and to patrons.

[copyright 2001; www.scecina.org/collection_policies.htm]

NOTES

1. Selection Criteria,"Collection Development Policies," Arizona State Library, Archives and Public Records website, www.dlapr.lib.az.us/cdt/colldev.htm.
2. Elizabeth Futas, ed., *Collection Development Policies and Procedures*, 3rd ed. (Phoenix, AZ: Oryx, 1995), 222.

Chapter Five

Format/Types of Materials Statement

A library's format statement generally refers to the types of information resources included—or *not* included—within its holdings. Although by no means a fixture in collection development policies, it is included as a response to one or more of the following issues:

- Delineation of the characteristics of those formats included in an institution's holdings
- Affirmation of the absence of media bias in the collection-building process.
- Citing limits to the acquisition of certain formats (as well as the rationale behind such restrictions)
- Documentation of specific features regarding the evaluation, acquisition, maintenance, servicing, and so forth of a particular medium

For some time, educators, librarians, and media experts in other fields have elaborated on the limitations of print resources—compared with other information formats—on the basis of criteria such as inherent appeal, effectiveness in communicating particular ideas and feelings, ease of use, timeliness, cost, availability, and durability.[1] Recognizing the limitations of a collection built exclusively around traditional print materials such as books and serials, some libraries (especially those serving educational institutions) operate under mandates to develop integrated multimedia holdings. Indeed, the American Library Association's *Information Power: Building Partnership for Learning*, the de facto professional source outlining school library standards, mandates integrated multimedia collections.

Perhaps the most concise—and open-ended—means of communicating receptivity to varied formats consists of a statement indicating that the library in question will acquire whatever information package is most appropriate to achieving institutional objectives. However, since many nonprint formats require specialized hardware for playback purposes (and additional equipment for reproduction, projection to groups, and other everyday applications), collection developers may feel it necessary to include more detail regarding the use of various software within the overall service scheme.

In addition to documenting a commitment to a broad range of media, libraries may find a format statement instrumental in clarifying the thrust of future acquisition priorities. G. Edward Evans, in his work *Developing Library and Information Center Collections*, addresses the pitfalls that a collection developer faces in attempting to select the most effective form of information package:

> With each passing year, as multimedia computer systems combine text, graphics, audio, and video clips, the distinction between books and audiovisuals becomes more and more blurred. Information that once was available only in printed formats is now available in several forms, including books, microfiche, CD-ROM, and online. Book publishers, especially publishers of scholarly journals, are thinking about and (in more and more cases) actually publishing their material electronically. Many publishers expect to use, and are using, CD-ROM packages to distribute reference material.[2]

Format limitations typically cited by libraries include (1) the limited availability of certain types of software, (2) obsolescence, and (3) equipment problems (e.g., high cost, complexity of operation, lack of dependability). These limitations are a product of the highly volatile marketplace and sheer diversity of nonprint media. The list below illustrates the diverse array of sound recordings commercially available during the life span of many presently employed librarians. This listing represents a comparatively small slice of the overall entertainment and educational media empire; the output of other sectors (film, video, micrographics, realia, etc.) presents an equally confusing picture.

AUDIO FORMATS MARKETED BETWEEN 1950–2000

- 78 rpm shellac discs (issued in a variety of sizes)
- Wire recordings (blank medium; spool sizes vary)
- Reel-to-reel magnetic tape (blank and prerecorded media; reel sizes vary)
- 45 rpm vinyl discs (varied sizes; primarily 7 inches in diameter)
- 33 rpm vinyl discs (varied sizes; primarily 12 inches in diameter)
- Soundpages/Soundsheets/Flexi-Discs/Talking Books (varied sizes and playback speeds)

- Audiocassettes (blank and prerecorded media; former available in three tape formulations as well as microcassette size)
- 8-track cassettes (blank and prerecorded media)
- Compact discs (3-inch and 5 1/2-inch sizes; various spin-off formats, including CD-Video, CD-Graphics, CD-Interactive, enhanced CDs, CD-Read Only Memory, CD-Recordable and CD-ReWritable)
- Digital audio tape (DAT)
- Digital compact cassettes (DCC)
- Mini-Discs (blank and prerecorded media)
- Digital Video Disc-Audio (blank and prerecorded media). Unlike DVDs, DVD-Audio releases are marketed directly to the audience for sound recordings; many other video formats—e.g., laserdiscs, 1/2-inch videotape formulations—include titles (concerts, documentaries, video clips, etc.) that emphasize audio information.

A number of factors—most notably, the rapid turnover of AV technologies driven by an innovative climate and unpredictability of media manufacturers and retailers regarding support of new products—have caused even the most open-minded, media-literate librarians to move cautiously before shifting their allegiance to up-and-coming formats. At the very least, the presence of outmoded formats in a collection places an added imperative on efficient weeding practices and creates the general impression that collection developers have failed to spend funds in the most effective manner.

Much information continues to be reissued in new formulations; for example, the work of popular music entertainer Al Jolson has probably been issued on virtually every graphic medium devised over the past 125 years. However, in cases where valuable material is available only on outmoded formats, some libraries may feel obligated to add new configurations to the existing collection rather than simply allowing one medium to supersede another. In short, the format statement should cover all issues emanating from the decision of the library to include (or not include) particular types of media. An in-depth treatment of format-related concerns might include responses to the following questions:

- How will playback equipment for essentially obsolete formats be maintained, repaired, and replaced?
- Are there any special concerns relating to storage (climate considerations, protective containers, display cases, etc.), handling, and maintenance? Will staff training (and clearly worded patron directives) be necessary to ensure that these concerns are properly addressed?
- Should particularly useful information available only on outmoded formats be copied to newer configurations? If so, are there any potential copyright violations?

- Should school libraries—typically not concerned with archival practices— consider shifting obsolete materials to institutions better equipped to handle special collections?
- Do evaluative criteria and acquisition sources of certain media vary to the extent that they should be separated from the general discussion of such matters in other portions of the policy?

SAMPLE POLICIES

While a substantial number of school library policies address all or most format-related concerns within a section referring in some manner to *types of material* (note the Aldine Independent School District and Baltimore County Public Schools excerpts below), some place such information under evaluative criteria, special collections, or a heading focusing exclusively on one configuration (e.g., serials, microforms). On the other hand, the Alemany High School policy covers media within the context of a long-range acquisitions plan.

Aldine Independent School District (Houston, Texas) Library Media Services Department

Policy and Procedures Manual

Types of Materials

BOOKS The basic collection should consist of reference works, books for curriculum support and enrichment, personal growth and recreational reading, and the teacher's resource (professional) collection.

BINDINGS

Elementary Schools: The district recommends pre-bound books except in cases where the publisher's library binding is guaranteed for the life of the pages. All "E" books and titles receiving heavy use should be pre-bound. Trade bindings are acceptable only in the teacher's resource or reference collection.

Secondary Schools: Although library bindings are preferred, schools may use trade bindings at the library media specialist's discretion. Trade bindings and paperback books are acceptable in any secondary collection when the title is needed and is only available in these bindings.

PERIODICALS All schools may order a limited number of magazines and newspapers which are paid for by the district. The number is consistent with the Texas State Library Standards for Learning Media Services. Additional magazines or newspapers may be ordered if funds are available in the school budget. Reference tools such as the *Reader's Guide*, *Book Review Digest*, and *Children's Magazine Guide* are not considered periodicals.

INFORMATION FILE MATERIALS   Information file materials consist of pamphlets, clippings, small maps, charts, tear sheets, small posters, pictures, etc. It is particularly useful for subject areas such as health, science, technology, and social sciences where students need more recent information than can sometimes be found in the book collection.

AUDIOVISUAL/NONPRINT MATERIALS   Software includes audio and video recordings, microforms, computer diskettes, multimedia kits, CD-ROMs, laser discs, and materials such as maps, globes, models, study prints, realia, games, and programmed instruction materials. Hardware consists of the equipment needed to read the various types of software. The audiovisual instructional materials in each school should be listed in the district online database and considered part of the resource collection regardless of the funding source. In some cases, materials such as maps and globes may be checked out for the school year to particular departments. Audiovisual hardware is recorded in the Library Media Center inventory. Some of the hardware may be loaned to teachers or departments on a long-term basis; it should be housed in the Library Media Center during summer vacation.

PAPERBACK BOOKS   Paperback books may be included in collections at all levels. Whether the library media specialist buys reinforced or regular paperbacks depends upon his or her judgment. Paperbacks are particularly useful for duplicate copies, titles of transient value, and as "book bait."

TRADE BOOKS   The elementary librarian is responsible for sets of trade books purchased by the district reading program directors for expanded literary enrichment. One barcode is assigned to each complete set. [revised June 1999; www.aldine.k12.tx.us]

Alemany High School (Mission Hills, California) Library

Collection Development Policy

Types of Materials Purchased   The Alemany High School Library updates its collection both annually and on a four-year cycle. These materials are purchased according to need and the wishes of parents and faculty members. These purchases also include those made in order to update class recommended reading lists.

TYPES OF MATERIALS UPDATED ANNUALLY   The Fiction Collection is updated according to the needs of the current class levels as well as changes in recommended reading lists. These reading lists are developed by the Librarians in association with the English Department.

TYPES OF MATERIALS UPDATED ACCORDING TO FOUR-YEAR CYCLE The Non-Fiction Collection is updated according to the needs of the Alemany High School Community. The Library is presently concentrating on updating the biography and literary criticism sections. Secondary priorities will include updating the space, science, and mathematics collection. These resources— and the remaining areas of the collection—will be kept current by means of a four-year purchasing cycle.

FOUR-YEAR PURCHASING CYCLE BREAKDOWN
Year One:

American History
Biographies
Literary Criticism
Social Science
U.S. Presidents

Year Two:

The Arts
Career Books
Literature
Philosophy
Religion
World Leaders

Year Three:

Drama and Plays
Mathematics
Science and Technology
Space Technology and Astronomy
World History

Year Four:

Country Studies
Geographical Materials
Foreign Language Materials
Multi-Cultural Materials
Poetry
Sports

[www.alemany.pvt.k12.ca.us/library/collection.html]

Baltimore County (Towson, Maryland) Public Schools

Selection Policy for School Library Media Center Collections

Considerations for Selection of Print Materials   There are general selection criteria which apply to all library media materials. The following media formats require additional considerations.

BOOKS   Due to the high cost of materials, it is important to examine books with the following additional criteria in mind before purchasing:

- Illustrations and layout
- Type style and text density
- Paper quality
- Durability of bindings
- Readability and interest levels
- Indexing

PAPERBACKS   Paperbacks are an inexpensive way to supplement the library media collection for duplication of titles, in-depth studies, special projects, and leisure reading. It is recommended that first copies of picture books be hardbacks.

When deciding whether to purchase paperback books or hardbound books, consider the following:

- Curricular demand placed on these books in the individual school
- Use of these materials for research, independent reading, duplication of classics, and popular fiction
- Cost and use of paperback books as compared to the cost of hardback books

PERIODICALS   Periodicals support the curriculum and provide leisure reading for students. Professional review journals and library periodicals for instruction may be considered for purchase. Consider access to full-text online periodical databases (e.g., ASAP[1] from Dialog Information Services).

NEWSPAPERS   Newspapers may be ordered as needed. Consider access to full-text online newspaper databases (e.g., *Baltimore Sun*, *New York Times*) from Dialog Information Services and the limited editions of the same titles on the World Wide Web.

PAMPHLETS   Pamphlets that support the curriculum may be added to the collection. It is recommended that they be organized in an information file by subject matter rather than fully cataloged. Apply general selection criteria.

REFERENCE   Reference materials in both print and electronic formats provide comprehensive information in both general and subject-specific areas.

They also serve as access tools to information from other sources including school, public, academic, and electronic collections.

The following points need to be considered:

- Cost effective in terms of projected use
- Authority
- Arrangement and indexing
- User-friendly

Selection of Nonprint Instructional Materials   Each curricular office is responsible for establishing an Instructional Materials Evaluation Committee as set forth in the Baltimore County Public Schools' selection policy statement. As part of the review process, an annual Instructional Materials and Technology Exhibit is held to showcase instructional materials for sale by various publishers/producers. The exhibit is open to all teachers, students, and citizens interested in previewing instructional materials.

The Office of Library and Information Technology establishes a Nonprint Evaluation Committee to preview and evaluate instructional materials which are being considered for inclusion in the *Library Instructional Media Catalog*. All materials listed in this catalog are approved for purchase. Library media specialists who wish to suggest titles for preview and evaluation should request these materials through the Office of Library and Information Technology Review and Evaluation Center.

CONSIDERATIONS FOR SELECTION OF NONPRINT MATERIALS   The criteria for selection of nonprint materials are essentially the same as for print materials. The quality of auditory and visual presentation should be considered as well as accuracy of information and the appropriateness of format.

Nonprint materials should:

- Promote instructional goals and support the curriculum
- Provide a variety of media formats to meet the needs of the curriculum
- Present content in appropriate format and acceptable technical quality
- Avoid dense text and graphics

CONSIDERATIONS FOR SELECTION OF ELECTRONIC RESOURCES   The criteria for selection of electronic resources are essentially the same as print materials. Electronic resources such as CD-ROM, computer software, and online services provide greater access to information. Access to these fee-based database services should be 24 hours a day with remote access from home. Availability of network versions and site license agreements are also factors in selection. See the evaluation form for detailed evaluation criteria developed for

the K–12 Maryland Digital Library Project, an initiative of the Maryland State Department of Education, Division of Library Development and Services.
Electronic resources should provide

- learner control through flexible pacing, variable difficulty, and optimal branching and linking;
- accurate and reliably maintained information;
- organization, searching capabilities, and navigation tools to enhance information retrieval;
- record keeping and management options, if applicable;
- readable text, attractive graphics, and an appealing layout;
- easy-to-understand, comprehensive documentation;
- user-friendly access; and
- 24-hour access with remote connection from home.

ACCESS TO INTERNET RESOURCES Access to the Internet is a right and privilege granted to all students by the Baltimore County Public Schools. Through the annual notification process of the Baltimore County Public School Discipline Code, parents or guardians will receive a booklet of all behavior expectations, including appropriate and safe use of the Internet. Parents or guardians who do not want their child to have access to Internet resources must submit a letter to the school principal. The Telecommunications Policy defines use of the Internet for "educational purposes," outlines expectations for appropriate and acceptable use, guidelines for school and office web publishing, and copyright compliance. [published July 1996; www.bcps.org/offices/lis/office/admin/selection.html]

NOTES

1. G. Edward Evans, *Developing Library and Information Center Collections*, 4th ed. (Englewood, CO: Libraries Unlimited, 2000), 273.

2. Evans, *Developing Library and Information Center Collections*, 273.

Chapter Six

Treatment of Specific Resource Groups

While format statements tend to discuss library media as a whole, many collection development policies include separate sections devoted to specific media formats. These sections may cover a wide range of concerns, such as selection criteria, acquisition issues, service imperatives, associated problems (e.g., preservation, hardware compatibility), and subcategories of interest to the library. Virtually any format found in library collections and archives might be emphasized in this manner; however, headings most frequently found in policies include serials, microforms, audiovisual resources (or more narrow media groupings, e.g., films, videotape, sound recordings), reference books, manuscripts, and government publications (covered in the next chapter). Electronic information has become an increasingly popular topic since the mid-1990s. Many libraries are likely to expand on the digital domain — perhaps focusing individually on various subtopics such as online commercial databases, laser optical software, computer software, floppy disks, and Internet websites — in future policy revisions.

SAMPLE POLICIES

Audiovisual Resources

University Laboratory High School (Urbana, Illinois) Library

Collection Development Policy
AV POLICY

1. The library provides AV materials and services for the following purposes:

- To supplement its collection of materials
- To implement, enrich, and support the curriculum of the school
- To meet the individual, educational, emotional, and recreational needs of students, faculty, and staff

2. Format

- The library's AV collection consists primarily of videos, but also includes art slides, electronic reference sources, and some audio materials.
- The library no longer collects filmstrips and does not collect music CDs.

[revised February 2000; last modified July 2001; www.uni.uiuc.edu/ library/policies/collectiondevelopment.html]

Electronic Information (See also Part II: Acceptable Use Policies)

University Laboratory High School Library (Urbana, Illinois)

Collection Development Policy

ELECTRONIC INFORMATION POLICY   In keeping with our role as a source of information, the library provides Internet access to information beyond the confines of our collection. The Internet affords us an exciting opportunity to have immediate access to timely and comprehensive information as well as a wide variety of primary sources. Providing connections to global information services and networks outside the library is different from selecting and purchasing materials for the library collection. The Internet changes rapidly, frequently, and unpredictably.

As the vast amount of information on the Internet is generated outside the library, the library cannot be responsible for accuracy, authenticity, currency, availability, or completeness of information. We cannot insure that Internet communications are secure or private.

Because of the library's limitations, the user is responsible for using discretion when considering the quality of material, questioning the validity of information, and choosing what is individually appropriate.

Through the required Computer Literacy curriculum, students are provided with guidelines for evaluating websites and search strategies for finding the most appropriate information from the Web. In addition, as students visit the library to conduct research on the Internet, they are trained how to use it in a responsible and discriminating manner.

In the University Laboratory High School Library setting, the Internet is a resource which provides timely access to students' information needs. Unfortunately, limited computer resources do not permit the library to support all types of Internet and computer usage. Therefore, in order to best allocate these finite resources, student use of the library's computers will be limited in the following ways:

- Academic use will always have priority over recreational use.
- Game playing, e-mail, chat, online shopping, personal "productivity" activities (e.g., word processing, web page development, etc.) and other inappropriate computer usage as determined by library staff are not permitted.
- Printing privileges are restricted to academic use. Exceptions to this policy will be made at the discretion of the librarian.

The library is also guided by existing institutional computer usage guidelines and the following American Library Association policy statements:

- *Access to Electronic Information, Services, and Networks*
- *Internet Questions and Answers*
- *Information on the Internet*

[revised February 2000; last modified July 2001; www.uni.uiuc.edu/library/policies/collectiondevelopment.html]

Textbooks

Northeast Community School District (Goose Lake, Iowa)

Instructional Materials Selection Policy
TEXT MATERIALS

A. At the time text adoption areas are determined, the appropriate teacher or teacher committee shall review materials and make recommendations concerning those materials.
B. Criteria for text materials shall be consistent with the general criteria for materials selection:

1. Materials shall support and be consistent with the general educational goals of the district and the objectives of specific courses.
2. Materials shall meet high standards of quality in factual content and presentation.
3. Materials shall be appropriate for the subject area and for the age, emotional development, ability level, and social development of the students for whom the materials are selected.

4. Materials shall have aesthetic, literary, or social value.

5. Materials chosen shall be by competent and qualified authors and producers.

6. Materials shall be chosen to foster respect for women, minorities, and ethnic groups, and shall realistically represent our pluralistic society, along with the roles and lifestyles open to both women and men in today's world. Materials shall be chosen to help students gain an awareness and understanding of the many important contributions made to our civilization by women, minorities, and ethnic groups. Materials shall clarify the multiple historical and contemporary forces with their economic, political, and religious dimensions. Materials shall be selected to motivate students and staff to examine their own attitudes and behaviors and to comprehend their own duties, responsibilities, rights, and privileges as participating citizens in a pluralistic, nonsexist society.

7. Materials shall be selected for their strengths rather than rejected for their weaknesses.

8. The selection of materials on controversial issues will be directed toward maintaining a balanced collection representing various views and to meet specific curriculum objectives.

9. Physical format and appearance of materials shall be suitable for their intended use.

C. Recommendations will be forwarded to the office of the superintendent through the principal in charge of the attendance center.

[www.iema-ia.org/IEMA101.html]

Chapter Seven

Special Collections

In the broadest sense, the term "special collections" refers to well-defined groupings of materials that stand in contrast with an institution's general holdings. Such collections typically exist to supplement the primary needs of a library's clientele.

Special collections presume the existence of the following conditions:

- adequate space for housing the materials;
- staff expertise;
- accessibility—via physical location and document delivery—to potential users;
- sufficient prestige to attract philanthropy and grants;
- a funding base adequate to subsidize facilities, maintenance, and use of archival resources; and
- the flexibility to shift collection building priorities to capitalize on recent acquisitions.

Whereas these resources often constitute the core holdings in museums, local historical societies, private foundations, professional associations, governmental agencies, and some academic and public libraries, schools tend to view the development of special holdings as something of a luxury. The costs of acquiring rare or hard-to-find resources combined with an emphasis on the chief archival tenets of security, limited access, and preservation are hard to justify given their peripheral relationship to the overriding educational mission of the school library. While only major federal archives (e.g., the Library of Congress, Smithsonian Institution), state libraries, and large public and university libraries will be able to afford diversified special collections, schools and/or other types of institutions possessing narrow subject interests are capable of developing outstanding specialized holdings. In addition to professional resources geared to staff needs, school libraries are a natural choice for housing documentation generated by institutional activities, including administrative planning; community programs; yearbooks, newsletters, and other publications; grant-related data; and so forth.

SAMPLE POLICIES

The excerpts below typify the special collections maintained by school libraries, most notably professional resources. In addition, the Longview Independent School District delineates its video holdings, whereas the University Laboratory High School Library provides a separate identity for its career materials.

Longview (Texas) Independent School District

Handbook of Policies and Procedures for Library Services K–12

District Media Services

PROFESSIONAL LIBRARY   The District Professional Library is housed in the Instructional Resource Center. Books, professional journals, instructional kits, and ESL materials can be checked out by L.I.S.D. personnel according to the following guidelines:

1. The circulation period lasts one month. Some items may be borrowed for a longer time frame with permission from the Library Supervisor with the understanding that they may be recalled, if needed.
2. There is a limit of ten titles per teacher.

VIDEO COLLECTION   The district collection of videotapes for grades K–8 and for in-service is housed in the Instructional Resource Center. Campus librarians annually receive a copy of the L.I.S.D. video catalog and are responsible for informing campus personnel about what is available through the IRC. A small number of videotapes are purchased for campus collections. Longview High School has an extensive collection of videotapes.

Instructional Television   As a member of the KERA Educational Consortium, L.I.S.D. makes use of instructional television programs from Channel 13. Teachers should adhere to the following procedures when requesting copies of ITV programs.

1. Using the Channel 13 Teacher Quick Reference Guide, select programs. Complete the top section of the "ITV Video Request" form. The anticipated show date may be more than one day; simply list all dates that the program will be needed.
2. All tape requests will be processed through the campus librarian. The librarian will review and mail all teacher requests to the IRC. This should be done at least 7 days prior to anticipated show date. Later requests will be accepted and filled if materials are available. As an occasional alternate, telephone requests will also be honored.
3. When the ITV Video Request form arrives at the IRC, it is logged and a notice of confirmation is sent to the requesting librarian.
4. Tapes will be sent from the IRC to the campus librarian, who will disburse to teachers. Teachers may pick up videotapes at the IRC if the request has already been mailed or called in. Notifying the IRC ahead of time will ensure that the tapes are ready for pickup. Many programs have to be copied prior to campus use and, therefore, are not immediately available.
5. After the taped program has been viewed, complete the evaluation section of the ITV Video Request form. Return videotape along with form to the campus librarian, who will then route it to the IRC.

Other Video Programs Video material other than ITV programs — including television fare, commercial videotapes, and copies of tapes brought by the teacher — may also be considered for classroom use if (1) they have instructional value, and (2) copyright guidelines (see Appendix A) are followed. To ensure that television programming is taped, teachers should complete the Video Program Request/Evaluation Form and submit it to either the campus librarian or district library supervisor. The portion of the form requesting air date and time does not have to be completed for nonbroadcast material; however, all other information should be submitted to the campus librarian when use of the video equipment is being scheduled. [1997–1998 edition; 1301 E. Young Street, Longview, TX 75602]

University Laboratory High School (Urbana, Illinois) Library

Collection Development Policy

Professional Collection In order to serve the needs of University Laboratory High School faculty and staff and other members of the University community, University Laboratory High School Library maintains a small professional collection of materials relating to the fields of education and library science.

The librarian selects titles appropriate for a core journal collection of interest and use to educators, administrators, and librarians, especially those at University Laboratory High School. In addition, key monographs in a few subject areas are acquired through selection or as gifts. These materials shall be subject to the selection criteria applying to the general collection.

Faculty and staff at University High School are invited to participate in the library's current contents service. Through this service, the library periodically provides table of contents of journals that would be of interest to individual faculty or staff members, thus allowing educators to stay abreast of current developments in their field.

University Laboratory High School faculty also have access to the much more comprehensive journal and monograph collections of the University Library's Education and Social Sciences Library.

College and Career Collection   The Library maintains a core collection consisting of *Peterson's Guide to Four-Year Colleges*, the *Occupational Outlook Handbook*, and a few other reference and circulating titles. The school's Student Services Office provides a larger collection of college and career guides, including standardized test preparation materials. [revised February 2000; last modified July 2001; www.uni.uiuc.edu/library/policies/collection development.html]

Chapter Eight

Resource Sharing

Resource sharing encompasses cooperative collection development and the delivery of documents and information through coordinated interlibrary efforts. Institutional cooperation has been facilitated in recent years by means of enhanced online capabilities—most notably, broadband communication and the proliferation of increasingly more powerful, comparatively inexpensive computers—and the development of faster and more efficient borrowing and lending systems. The American Library Association's *Guide to Cooperative Collection Development* cites the following benefits of library cooperation in collection building:

1. Promotion of more systematic collection development planning to permit calculated responses when library income becomes flat or decreases
2. Elimination of undesirable redundancy in development of collections of the future of distribution of responsibility for certain subject areas or material formats
3. Ability of some libraries to exercise greater selectivity in some areas and the consequent acquisition of fewer noncore titles because of the knowledge that these titles will be available through resource sharing
4. Coordination of retention policies for little-used materials, last copy, serial backfiles, etc.
5. Coordination of preservation among libraries to reduce redundancy of expensive preservation activities
6. Improved staff knowledge, ability, and skills for local collection development, especially when a cooperative program includes a strong training component and there is frequent communication among staff of the cooperating libraries[1]

A resource-sharing statement within the written policy typically describes one or more of the activities at the core of the cooperative arrangements between libraries. Typical programs include

- shared purchase of particular kinds of items;
- distributed collection development responsibilities;
- cooperative retention;
- cooperation to complete a single project (e.g., a serials union list, storage project, weeding project); and
- cooperation in areas associated with collection development (e.g., cataloging, preservation projects, automation programs, special interlibrary loan agreements).[2]

It is imperative that cooperative collection development agreements be described in the written policy, whether in the community background statement, the appendixes, or a separate section. Elizabeth Futas provides a rationale for including the text (or at least a summary) of such contracts:

> Some materials are not purchased because a member of the consortia already has them or has promised to purchase them, and the library must purchase some materials because it has commitments to the consortia. Library patrons have the right to know what effects such arrangements have on them and the use of their library and any member library's collections.[3]

SAMPLE POLICIES

The policy excerpts included here reflect the fact that formalized school media center resource-sharing programs tend to be more limited in scope than those developed by other types of libraries. The Atwater policy reflects the commitment to district-wide cooperation found in many North American schools. The document also cites the general predisposition to work with institutions outside the district in order to meet student needs. On the other hand, the Wilmington policy places an emphasis on statewide interlibrary loan initiatives.

Atwater (California) Elementary School District
Selection Policy for Books and Materials

Interlibrary Loan   Each media center is a part of a total district library program. Cooperation with other libraries may be necessary to avoid duplication of expensive items and to share items otherwise unavailable. Efforts should be made to encourage interlibrary loans to provide for the needs of students at all levels. [adopted 1990; http://mse.aesd.k12.ca.us/library/selectpol .html]

Wilmington (Vermont) School District

Collection Development Policy

Resource Sharing/Interlibrary Loan   It is the intent of the Board of Education that Wilmington Middle/High School will use standard library format (MARC) for all items included in the library's collection, and that the school will continue to participate in the Vermont Union Catalog and K12Cat, and will adhere to the Vermont Interlibrary Loan (ILL) Code and the School Guidelines for Use of the Department of Library Resources. (These documents are on file in the media centers.) [www.dves.k12.vt.us/Users/cethier/ libpol.html]

NOTES

1. Bart Harloe, ed., *Guide to Cooperative Collection Development* (Chicago: American Library Association, 1994), 3–4.

2. Harloe, *Guide to Cooperative Collection Development*, 7.

3. Elizabeth Futas, ed., *Collection Development Policies and Procedures*, 3rd ed. (Phoenix, AZ: Oryx, 1995), 253.

Chapter Nine

Selection Aids

Selection aids function as a guide for librarians in deciding which resources to add to the collection. G. E. Gorman and B. R. Howes state that an effective selection tool should do either or both of two things:

1. It must identify the item, and provide the selector with enough information to determine what the item is (i.e., it must act as an "alerting device)."
2. It must evaluate the item, or tell the selector whether the item is any good for its stated purpose, and if it is not, in what particulars it fails (i.e., it must act as an "evaluating device"[1])

Although not always listed in written policies, libraries rely most heavily on the following types of selection aids:

- Bibliographies
  A. Evaluative Bibliographies
    1. subject bibliographies
       a. total coverage
       b. selective
    2. standard lists
       a. current
       b. retrospective
       c. out-of-print lists
    3. guides to the literature
    4. library catalogs

    B. Alerting Bibliographies
       1. national bibliographies
       2. trade bibliographies
- Reviews
    A. Guides
       1. digests
       2. indexes
    B. Journals
       1. general
       2. subject specialist journals
       3. library journals
       4. specialist book selection journals
       5. newspapers
- Advertising
    A. Display Advertisements
    B. Direct Mail
    C. Advance Notices[2]

The arguments for including a section on selection resources within the collection development statement include the following:

- the section establishes a benchmark for consistency in the use of these tools;
- it assists new staff in adapting to a library's established selection procedures; and
- it communicates the level of professionalism involved in the evaluation process to the community at large.

In addition to listing useful published resources, some policies note the more specialized strategies employed by collection developers, for example, consideration of purchase requests from library clientele.

SAMPLE POLICIES

The contrast in approaches—between merely citing selection tools (see The Nueva School) and a more comprehensive approach, including broader concerns relating to the evaluation process (see St. Joseph School)—is apparent in the following policy excerpts. The chapter dealing with acquisitions also covers selection tools—both in the introduction and sample policies—at length.

SAMPLE POLICIES

Nueva School (Lamont, California) Library

Selection Policy

Selection Tools   The following lists and tools shall be consulted in the selection of materials, but resources are not limited to these listings:

A. Bibliographies, using the latest editions and supplements

American Historical Fiction
Basic Book Collection for Elementary Grades
The Best in Children's Books
The Bookfinder
Children and Books
Children's Catalog
Elementary School Library Collection
European Historical Fiction and Biography
From A to Zoo
Guide to Sources in Educational Media
Junior High School Catalog
Reference Books for School Libraries
Senior High School Catalog
Subject Guide to Children's Books in Print
Subject Index to Books for Intermediate Grades
Subject Index to Books for Primary Grades
(as well as special bibliographies, prepared by educational organizations
    for particular subject matter areas)

B. Current reviewing media

AAAS Science Books and Films
ACL Review
American Film & Video Association Evaluations
Book Links
Booklist
Bulletin of the Center for Children's Books
CD-ROM World
English Journal
Gifted Child Quarterly
Horn Book
Kliatt
Language Arts

Library Journal
Reading Teacher
Roeper Review
School Library Journal

[approved by the Board of the Nueva School, February 2, 1994; The Nueva School, 6565 Skyline Blvd., Hillsborough, CA 94010]

St. Joseph School (Seattle, Washington)

Our Collection

Selection Guidelines   The selection and evaluation process of library materials is guided by the collection development policy of the school. This policy also reflects the *Library Bill of Rights*, as adopted by the American Library Association, and the guidelines for the school library media programs of the Catholic Archdiocese of Seattle and the State of Washington. The policy includes the following factors:

- Supporting and enriching the curriculum
- Supporting personal and recreational needs of the students
- Reflecting quality of content and artistic merit
- Reflecting religious, ethnic, social, and economic diversity
- Reflecting various points of view, timeliness, permanence, and importance of subject matter
- Reflecting age appropriateness
- Reflecting the reputation of author and publisher
- Creating a balanced collection covering a broad range of subjects

The following tools and resources are used or consulted when making selections:

- *School Library Journal*
- Puget Sound Council for the Review of Children's Media—monthly meetings
- *Book Links* (magazine)
- Book awards

  - Caldecott
  - Newbery
  - Young Reader's Choice
  - Coretta Scott King

- American Library Association's Notable Books
- Others

- *New York Times Book Review*
- Teacher, student, and parent recommendations
- Catholic School Librarians Group meetings
- *Children's Catalog* (Wilson)
- *Junior High School Catalog* (Wilson)
- Bibliographies

    - American Library Association
    - Seattle Public Library
    - Other Schools
    - University of Washington School of Information and Library Science course bibliographies
    - List of books from the ACLU
    - Other organizations

- Publisher's representatives
- Book stores
- Reputable publisher and dealer catalogs

Through the curriculum, particular emphasis is placed on the recognition of the ethnic diversity of our society. To adequately expand the collection in order that it reflect this diversity, the following special bibliographies and book lists are consulted:

- *African American Images Catalog* (Book Distributors)
- *Against Borders: Promoting Books for a Multicultural World* (H. Rockman)
- *Black History Catalog* (Empak Publishing Co.)
- Other book lists emphasizing multicultural books

[www.stjosephsea.org/library/collectn.htm]

NOTES

1. G. E. Gorman and B. R. Howes, *Collection Development for Libraries* (London: Bowker-Saur, 1990), 249.
2. Gorman and Howes, *Collection Development for Libraries*, 248.

Chapter Ten

Acquisitions

Acquisitions relates to locating and obtaining those materials determined to be desirable additions to a library collection. A substantial number of written policies do not include a separate acquisitions section. One perspective holds that the process is not directly concerned with collection building; rather, it is a business-oriented support function better placed in the library's procedure manual. In this context, school librarians are likely to rely heavily upon the services of the district's purchasing department. Other experts advocate a more holistic view. G. Edward Evans argues,

> Collection development and acquisitions have always been closely coordinated, if not integrated, in libraries and information centers with successful programs. In today's increasingly electronic environment, that coordination/integration becomes vital.[1]

Few professionals acquainted with the intricacies of acquisitions work would question its importance to a sound collection management program. According to Joyce Ogburn, acquisitions personnel are best qualified to

> [assess] the risk and feasibility of acquisition, the availability of the resources, and the chances of success; control the system and methods needed, the choice of the source, the supporting services, and the resources themselves; and quantify the resources, work, and costs involved to conduct the business of acquisitions and measures of success.[2]

School librarians—who are educated, first and foremost, to be teaching specialists—may lack the acquisitions skills of personnel hired to work in the typically larger, more diversified academic and public library settings. Accordingly, they generally find it advisable to cultivate a close working relationship with district specialists. The policy should document such functional roles as a means of assuring the integrity of library prerogatives.

The basic functions of the acquisitions process include document requests, bibliographic verification, order preparation, allocation and encumbrance of funds, vendor purchase orders, outstanding order files, processing of invoices, adjustment of fund accounts, processing of incoming materials, and forwarding materials to the cataloging department.[3] Those libraries addressing some aspect of acquisitions in their written policies tend to focus on order sources or vendor relationships (e.g., type of buying plans employed). Perhaps due to its perception as a support service, acquisitions functions—if covered—are often outlined within other sections of the policy, most notably Evaluative Criteria, Selection Aids, Funding, and Formats.

SAMPLE POLICY

Aldine Independent School District (Houston, Texas) Library Media Services Department

Policy and Procedures Manual

Ordering LMC Materials—Directives from the Business Office

1. Please do not send catalog pages to the business office for ordering unless it's an order form from the catalog.
2. When typing an attachment, use a spreadsheet or database program and create columns for author, title, order number, quantity, and price. Sort in alphabetical order by author or title.
3. Magazine and newspaper orders are sent to the Director of Library Media Services
4. We are strongly discouraging you from accepting preview books from publishers.
5. All materials (book/audio-visual) must be shipped to central receiving when ordered.

Ordering Books and AV

1. Consult the book bid manual. Orders should be placed with lowest bid company possible.

2. Follow the instruction in the Library Bid Manual for completing requisition correctly.
3. Using Filemaker Pro, click on Vendor Requisitions.
4. Select New Requisition.
5. Enter funding codes. Coding at the top of the page should be as follows:

	Fund	Agency	Organization	Activity	Function	Object
Books						
AV						
Bindery						

6. Complete the remainder of the form following the example shown. If ordering more items than will fit on the form, type a separate list, in alphabetical order by title, and attach it to the vendor requisition. Use the following commodity codes when ordering materials:

Products	Commodity Codes
Compact discs	65020
Periodicals	12003
Etc.	

7. On the vendor requisitions, list barcodes, automated processing, and security tags on separate lines.
8. Include shipping and handling for all orders from vendor not on the bid list (shipping from book bid vendors is free).
9. Print the requisition by clicking the print button at the top of the vendor requisition. Select "Current Record" and click OK.
10. Return to Main Menu. Select Ledger. Select page layout for Landscape view. Fill in object code that was at the bottom of the requisition. Print. Note: only one ledger is needed when sending multiple orders from the same fund.
11. Obtain the principal's signature and sign your name on the second line of the requisitions. Both signatures must be in blue ink.
12. Put together vendor requisition, item list (if there is one), vendor specifications, book specification, and local holdings format and make two copies of each page.
13. Staple each set together in the upper left-hand corner. Take the original set and one copy, assemble, and staple them together in the middle. Send these, along with one copy of the ledger sheet (see appendixes) to the Director of Library Media Services.
14. Keep the other copy for your files.

PROCESSING OF BOOKS AND AV MATERIALS CHECKLIST

- Write date of arrival on box.
- Check off books received on purchase order.
- Check physical condition of each book. Note any imperfections.
- Optional: Write source information on title page along spine margin (i.e., date of arrival, company, net price, and P.O. number).
- Label with I.D. stamp on the following portion of the book:

  1. Inside front cover
  2. Inside back cover
  3. Title page
  4. Edges of pages

- If needed, apply title stamp:

  1. Inside front cover
  2. Inside back cover
  3. Title page

- Librarian downloads vendor disks to Mitinet MARC and checks for additions and corrections.
- Export files to a disk labeled with school name, file name, and number of records. Send the disk to the Library Systems Administrator. When the disk is returned, check the catalog to be certain records have loaded correctly.

Optional processing, if needed:

- Stick label on book spine or book jacket one inch up from bottom of book and cover with label protector, clear book tape, or mylar cover.
- Affix mylar cover over book jacket or book cover (optional).
- Glue book pocket inside back cover. Place all cards in pocket. If the mylar jacket is in the way, place pocket on nearest end page.
- Glue book blurbs inside front cover or end page (optional).

Ordering Periodicals   Periodicals are ordered once a year. The district contracts with a jobber. The Director of Library Media Services will send a catalog of available periodicals to each school. The library media specialist will select titles in accordance with the numbers allocated by the district. The library media specialist will return the list to the Director of Library Media Services by the stated deadline. Once subscriptions have been submitted, the library media specialist will report any problems (i.e., missing issues or lapsed subscriptions) to the jobber. All renewals are handled through the jobber; the librarian should not respond to renewal notices from individual periodicals.

The current allocations for periodicals are as follows:

- Elementary School   10 student titles; 5 professional titles
- Intermediate School   1 title/25 students; 8 professional titles
- Middle School   1 title/25 students; 8 professional titles
- Ninth Grade   1 title/25 students; 8 professional titles
- High School   1 title/25 students; 10 professional titles

Ordering Newspapers   The district newspaper allotment is as follows as per Aldine Administrative Policies Handbook:

- Elementary School   1 local newspaper
- Intermediate School   3 newspapers (1 must be local)
- Middle School   3 newspapers (1 must be local)
- Ninth Grade   4 newspapers (1 must be local)
- High School   5 newspapers (1 must be local)

When ordering the *Houston Chronicle*, type days, quantity, and price on school letterhead stationary. When ordering any other newspaper, try to use a district jobber. If not working with a jobber, order directly from the publication by filling out a requisition following Aldine acquisition procedures.

Ordering Rebound Books with Bindery Funds

1. Submit request for binder funds to the Director of Library Media Services through e-mail or on letterhead stationery.
2. Prepare requisition using local book instructions.
3. Do not contact or send books to the bindery until you receive copies of the green and white purchase orders.
4. Follow the procedures below for the different binder companies.

[revised June 1999; www.aldine.k12.tx.us]

NOTES

1. G. Edward Evans, *Developing Library and Information Center Collections*, 4th ed. (Englewood, CO: Libraries Unlimited, 2000), 314.

2. Joyce L. Ogburn, "T2: Theory in Acquisition Revisited," *Library Acquisitions Practice and Theory* 21 (Summer 1997): 168.

3. G. Edward Evans and Sandra M. Heft, *Introduction to Technical Services*. 6th ed. (Englewood, CO: Libraries Unlimited, 1994), 23. Also reproduced as a figure in Evans, *Developing Library and Information Center Collections*, 318.

Chapter Eleven

Gifts

Many school librarians tend to go too far in accepting donated resources, relaxing the evaluative criteria to a considerably greater extent than as applied to traditional library purchases. They generally do so either to please would-be donors or to compensate for budgetary shortfalls. This practice opens the floodgates for patrons and others to demand the inclusion of additional materials of poor quality, albeit often at considerable cost.

Even when gifts are added to the collection according to the same standards applied to purchased items, accepting gifts poses myriad problems:

- Free items are not really free in that they require investments of time and money to process.
- Donations often come with strings attached: for example, libraries may be required to take an entire collection (rather than being allowed title-by-title discretion) or house it in a special facility. A particularly strong collection typically commits the institution to future acquisitions. This consideration generally falls outside the capabilities and reach of school collections.
- Even where gifts meet evaluative criteria, the donation of large numbers of titles within a relatively narrow subject area often results in an unbalanced collection.
- Donors may well be offended if the library refuses their gift or, worse yet, disposes of the material in a manner they don't approve of (e.g., book sale, public giveaway, incineration).

Some libraries choose to refuse all gifts rather than inherit any of these problems. Other institutions opt to limit gifts to financial endowments. In this manner, the library enjoys greater control over the particular acquisitions to its collection. Nameplates within individual books, honorary plaques, and the naming of libraries and special collections represent strategies employed by librarians to encourage monetary gifts.

Whatever choices the library makes, it is imperative that they be codified in a written policy statement. The statement ought to incorporate clear-cut evaluative criteria, or allude to a listing elsewhere in the policy. Step-by-step procedures for handling gifts should also be included along with a mechanism for contacting donors about materials that the library declines to place in the collection. Libraries should spell out the means by which unacceptable materials are disposed of, and such actions should take place only with the prior understanding—and granted permission—of the donor. This is most effectively secured by means of a donor agreement form to be read and signed prior to the actual delivery of the gift.

A truly thorough gifts policy will also note target audiences likely to provide the most valuable donations (including collection building monies) along with strategies for reaching them. A periodic newsletter (print or online) represents a useful public relations tool that can stimulate focused gift giving (i.e., geared to perceived institutional needs) through announcements of recent donations or by profiling the library's primary objectives.

ACQUISITIONS ISSUES

While a separate section within the overall policy helps focus attention on the process of handling gifts, it is important to include provisions within the other collection development components that are also affected by this program. Acquisitions is the sector perhaps most directly involved in terms of the expenditure of staff time and effort. The receipt of donations often entails the maintenance of an active exchange program administered by the department (or staff) charged with processing incoming material.

Two types of exchanges are typically employed by libraries to dispose of unwanted items. One consists of preparing a list of unwanted titles and sending it (usually via e-mail) to other libraries, first within the school district. Libraries can trade materials, or the institution requesting a particular item may simply be assessed the shipping cost. The other method, albeit less widely used in school libraries due to the limited value of materials typically acquired from donors, involves selling titles to a dealer in rare and out-of-print books. The transaction usually involves the dealer issuing an agreed-upon amount of credit to the library that can be applied to later purchases.

SAMPLE POLICIES

The policy excerpts below reflect the differing approaches taken by various institutions. The Aldine Independent School District emphasizes its receptivity to donations, whereas the School District of Philadelphia focuses on its commitment to applying the same criteria to gifts as in the case of regular purchases.

Aldine Independent School District (Houston, Texas) Library Media Services Department

Policy and Procedures Manual

Gifts   The district accepts anything cheerfully, but reserves the right to determine its usefulness. Library media specialists receiving gifts of books should have an agreement with the donor as to the disposition of materials, which may be judged inappropriate for the school collection. In most cases, they may be given to other libraries in the district of the community. Donated materials must meet the same criteria as those selected for purchase. They will not be placed in a special collection, since past experience has shown that limits their usefulness. Books may be given a bookplate acknowledging the donor. Donor slips should be given to the donor and duplicates kept in the Library Media Center records. A letter of appreciation from the Library Media Center and/or the school should be sent to the donor. The library media specialists may wish to place donated books on display before they are placed in circulation. If the donor wishes, the library media specialist will gratefully accept gifts of money with the provision that the librarian is allowed to make the selection or give the donor a list from which he may choose. Gifts of magazines or other types of materials will be accepted on the same basis as the books. [revised June 1999; www.aldine.k12.tx.us]

School District of Philadelphia Library Programs and Services

Selection Policy for School Library Materials

Criteria For Gifts And Unsolicited Materials   Gifts and unsolicited materials must meet the following general selection criteria in order to be accepted and become a part of the school library collection:

1. They must support and be consistent with the general educational goals of the state and district and the aims and objectives of the individual schools and specific courses.

2. They must meet high standards of quality in factual content, artistic and literary value, and presentation.
3. They must be current and up-to-date.
4. They must be appropriate for the subject area and for the age, emotional development, ability level, learning styles, and social development of students for whom materials are selected.
5. Physical format and appearance of these materials must be suitable for their intended use.
6. They must help students gain an awareness of our diverse society.

[revised February 5, 2002; www.libraries.phila.k12.pa.us/misc/selection-policy.html]

Chapter Twelve

Budgeting/Funding

Although a core feature of collection management, the allocation of funds has only recently become a fixture in policy statements. In *Collection Development Policies and Procedures*, Elizabeth Futas attributes this change to the following factors:

- processes once carried out behind closed doors are now appearing in public documents; and
- procedures once a part of manuals attached to policy documents are today more likely to be inserted into the policy proper.[1]

The rationale for discussing collection allocations within policies is twofold:

- increased calls for accountability on the part of public institutions; and
- the desire of library administrators for ammunition in budgetary hearings.[2]

In order to be effective, the funding section should focus on the sources for the materials budget, whether or not supplementary monies are available, and the basic breakdowns for acquiring library holdings. This involves addressing the following questions (sometimes located elsewhere in the policy):

- Exactly what kinds of resources are being purchased through mainstream budgetary allotments?
- How does the library determine its collection priorities?
- Assuming essential services are in no way compromised, can funds be saved by substituting one format for another?

- Will a cooperative acquisitions program facilitate fiscal savings?
- Has the library made a reasonable effort to obtain support through grants, philanthropy, and other outside sources?

A problematic undercurrent to the funding statement is the inclusion of extraneous procedural details and complicated allocation formulas, which detract from the essential information required for public consumption. Extensive line-item breakdowns and thoroughgoing discussions of performance-based budgets are better placed in an all-encompassing procedures manual.

SAMPLE POLICIES

School media centers lag well behind other types of libraries in providing the type of budgetary information cited above. The Aldine Independent School District provides a general outline of the sources for collection building funds, but does not address any specific concerns such as how funding affects choice of media formats, cooperative acquisitions, and the like. On the other hand, the Longview Independent School District policy limits its coverage of funding to guidelines addressing the receipt and expenditure of fines for overdue and lost materials.

Aldine Independent School District (Houston, Texas) Library Media Services Department
Policy and Procedures Manual

Use of Funds
LOCAL FUNDS   Money for Library Media Center books and audio-visual software from the district budget is allocated on a per capita or on a special needs basis at the beginning of each year. Local budget money left on a school's account on August 31 of each year automatically reverts to the district's general fund.

BINDERY FUNDS   Money for rebinding library books may be requested from the Director of Library Media Services. Make sure the bindery budget request is on school letterhead stationery stating the dollar amount needed with the library media specialist's signature.

FEDERAL FUNDS   Federal monies are given to designated schools on the basis of need and are often intended for special purposes, programs, or curriculum areas. Schools are notified of these allocations as soon as possible after the district receives approval from the Texas Education Agency. The federal government sets the time limit for spending these amounts.

NOTIFICATIONS OF FUNDS   Building principals and library media specialists are informed about their allocations by the Director of Library Media services. Money is designated for special services; this information is included in the notification. A monthly statement of expenditures is provided to each campus library by the business office.

OTHER FUNDS   Other sources of money are sometimes available at the building level from the campus principal's budget, book fairs, fundraisers, the PTA, or occasionally from donors within the community.

FUNDRAISING PROJECTS   Library media specialists may conduct a book fair if they receive permission from the principal.

FINES   Secondary and intermediate schools usually allow their respective library media centers to use money received from book fines; elementary schools do not charge fines for overdue books. Overdue book fines are assessed at ten cents per day.

LOST OR DAMAGED BOOKS   Money paid for lost books is used for replacements. [revised June 1999; www.aldine.tx.us]

Longview (Texas) Independent School District

Handbook of Policies and Procedures for Library Services K–12

Fines and Payment for Lost Books
FINES

1. In elementary schools, it is preferable that a pupil not be allowed to check out other books until the ones previously charged to him have been returned. Exceptions may be made as the librarian sees fit, especially if students need materials for assignment. Fines are collected in the elementary school at the discretion of the campus librarian and principal. If fines are charged, the amount is two cents per day.
   a. Students who owe more than $1.00 may check out material only with permission from the librarian.
   b. All fines are exclusive of Saturdays, Sundays, and holidays.
   c. Absence excuses a student from payment of a fine only if book is returned the first day that the student is back.
   d. The maximum fine for an overdue book is $1.00 per item.
   e. Elementary school students are usually limited to checking out one book at a time, subject to the librarian's discretion.
2. In middle schools, fines for late returns are five cents per day.
   a. Students who owe more than $1.00 may check out material only with permission from the librarian.

   b. All fines are exclusive of Saturdays, Sundays, and holidays.

   c. Absence excuses a student from payment of a fine only if the book is returned the first day that the student is back at school.

   d. The maximum fine is $1.00 per item.

3. In Longview High School, fines for late returns are as follows: five cents per day for fourteen-day loans and five cents per pound for overnight or reference books.

   a. All fines are exclusive of Saturdays, Sundays, and holidays.

   b. Absence does not excuse a student from payment of a fine.

   c. The maximum fine is $3.00 per item.

   d. Students with library fines and overdue books may not check out a book.

4. The librarian may allow students to render some library service in lieu of paying a library fine in case of extreme financial straits.

PAYMENT FOR LOST BOOKS

1. In elementary and middle schools, students will be charged the original cost of the book, rounded to the next higher dollar value, for books that are lost or damaged beyond repair. Minimum charge is $4.00. At the Longview High School library, students will be charged the replacement cost for lost or destroyed books.

2. The librarian, principal, and homeroom teacher may use their combined discretion in exempting a student from paying for a lost book in case of extreme financial problems. Some library or school service may be accepted in lieu of payment.

3. If a lost and paid-for book is found, the fine due at the time the book was paid for is deducted from the cost of the book. The remaining amount is returned to the student who checked out the book.

PAYMENT FOR DAMAGED BOOKS

1. This category includes, but is not limited to, books that have been water soaked, books with missing pages, books with torn pages that have been improperly mended, and books with more than ten pages of pen or crayon marking defacement rendering the book irreparable. Elementary school students will be charged the original price of the book with a $4.00 minimum. Secondary school students will pay the replacement cost rounded to the nearest dollar.

2. Cover damage (replacement of cover necessary)—$6.00 rebinding fee.

3. Cover damage (minor)—$2.00.

4. Pencil marks—student will completely erase all marks or be charged $.25 per page.

5. Crayon or ink marks—$.50 per page up to the price of the book.
6. Torn page—$.50 (Student should bring page to librarian to mend.)

EXPENDITURE OF FINE MONIES

1. The librarian decides whether to replace a lost book with the same edition of a title or some newer and/or more relevant title, or material in an entirely different category.
2. Fine funds may be disbursed as the librarian chooses to improve that particular library.
3. Expenditures of fine monies should be documented in ledger form, with receipts available for audit purposes.

UNPAID-FOR LOST BOOKS At the end of the current school year, if a student has lost a book and has not paid for it, a statement is attached to the student's permanent record card in the registrar's office. This statement indicates the author, title, and price of the book lost and is signed by the librarian. If the student has withdrawn from school prior to the end of school, this statement is attached at the time of withdrawal. [1997–1998 edition; 1301 E. Young Street, Longview, TX 75602]

NOTES

1. Elizabeth Futas, ed., *Collection Development Policies and Procedures*, 3rd ed. (Phoenix, AZ: Oryz, 1995), 199.
2. Futas, *Collection Development Policies and Procedures*, 199.

Chapter Thirteen

Intellectual Freedom

The very existence of this book presumes the importance of a written collection development policy, produced in a collaborative manner and authorized by administrative units such as a school board, superintendent, director of technology or library services, and key site supervisors, most notably the principal. However, more than three decades of observing and discussing the phenomenon of library censorship has convinced us that the presence of an official collection development document tends to possess limited value as a deterrent to the attempted suppression of books and other materials. Administrators — who can legitimately argue that the final responsibility for decisions relating to the acquisition of library resources, as well as patron access to these resources, rests in their hands — are hesitant to delegate decision making to subordinates (no matter how qualified and well informed) such as the head librarian. In cases where the librarian acts as a conduit for simply passing on recommendations to the governing official, the latter is somewhat defensive about appearing to override or contradict such advice. Whether motivated by public intimidation, a desire to effectively dispatch a public relations headache, or a clear-cut sense of the ethical issues involved, administrators tend to rationalize that they are best situated to understand the bigger picture. They argue that if the constitutional underpinnings of American citizenship "take a hit," then so be it. After all, they ask, is one problematic decision likely to have a long-term impact on the integrity of American democracy? In their minds, it is far easier to resolve the immediate crisis than to face the prolonged repercussions likely to ensue from a stout defense of controversial materials. Such conflicts have the potential to threaten institutional credibility, job security, and the cohesiveness of the community at large.

With the possible exception of small public libraries, schools — both public and private — are generally most vulnerable to arbitrary decision making on the part of upper-level governance. Administrators representing these institutions are most likely to submit to community demands due to a direct dependence on local funding and administrative oversight.

In part due to their placement within a more decentralized environment, academic and special librarians often possess greater autonomy in deciding matters of intellectual freedom. Furthermore, academic librarians are insulated by a number of principles residing at the fundamental core defining institutions of higher learning: (1) the library is the center of the institution's teaching and research activities; (2) academic freedom is essential to the integrity of the educative process; and (3) administrators within academia tend to have been educators themselves—even regents are usually well-educated products of this system.

Due to the diversity of their respective work environments (e.g., corporations, small businesses, governmental agencies, law offices, health-care facilities, mass media entities), special librarians are somewhat harder to assess. However, the narrow focus of the organizations they serve (often staffed by highly trained professionals) and noncontroversial nature of the information typically acquired, organized, and disseminated by the library confers secondary status upon intellectual freedom concerns.

The key factor determining the degree to which school librarians are permitted input into decisions regarding intellectual freedom appears to rest more on professional intangibles than whether or not a written policy is in place. The opinions of a librarian possessing both a proven track record in executing library functions and a collegial relationship with administrators and staff possess the best chance of influencing administrative decision making. Above all, administrators are concerned with facilitating effective organizational operations and minimizing criticism from within and without the institution. Librarians who are able to assist in achieving these goals will be valued members of any administrator's inner circle.

As part of its overall recommendation that the facets of the collection-building program be documented in a written policy, the American Library Association identifies two sections relating specifically to intellectual freedom. These are outlined in the following manner within the *Intellectual Freedom Manual*:

Policy on Controversial Materials (section V within Part 1: Selection of Library Materials)
    A. General Statement
    B. Library Bill of Rights
    C. Freedom to Read

Procedures for Dealing with Challenged Materials
    A. Request for Review
    B. The Review Committee
    C. Resolution and Appeal[1]

The *Intellectual Freedom Manual* advises that the collection development policy "address problems associated with the acquisition of controversial materials." The general statement should set the tone for these sections, noting the relevance of intellectual freedom to librarianship. Those libraries attempting to provide a philosophical stance on this matter generally include an affirmation of the Library Bill of Rights. While some institutions may consider reference to additional documents to be redundant, others may incorporate resources that either reinforce intellectual freedom principles or focus on particular issues. Frequently employed materials include the Freedom to Read statement, the ALA's Policy on Confidentiality of Library Records, and the text of the First Amendment to the U.S. Constitution.

Since the Library Bill of Rights was approved by the ALA Council at the 1939 Annual Conference in San Francisco, the ALA has on occasion received requests from within the profession for further clarification of its stance regarding intellectual freedom. In response to such concerns, the ALA's Intellectual Freedom Committee has drafted many additional documents aimed at providing additional guidance to librarians confronted with censorship issues. Among the more notable (and still useful) of these documents are the following:

- Access to Electronic Information, Services, and Networks (adopted January 24, 1996)
- Access to Library Resources and Services Regardless of Gender or Sexual Orientation (adopted June 30, 1993)
- Challenged Materials (adopted June 25, 1971; last amended January 10, 1990)
- Diversity in Collection Development (adopted July 14, 1982; amended January 10, 1990)
- Economic Barriers to Information Access (adopted June 30, 1993)
- Evaluating Library Collections (adopted February 2, 1973; amended July 1, 1981)
- Exhibit Spaces and Bulletin Boards; Meeting Rooms (adopted July 2, 1991)
- Expurgation of Library Materials (adopted February 2, 1973; last amended January 10, 1990)
- Free Access to Libraries for Minors (adopted June 30, 1972; last amended July 3, 1991)
- Library-Initiated Programs as a Resource (adopted January 27, 1982; amended June 26, 1990)
- Restricted Access to Library Materials (adopted February 2, 1973; last amended July 3, 1991)
- Statement on Labeling (adopted July 13, 1951; last amended June 26, 1990)
- Universal Right to Free Expression (adopted January 16, 1991)

The ALA encourages libraries to incorporate these policy statements into their respective philosophies of library service as needed. (They can be found at the ALA website, www.ala.org.)

The ALA has also formulated a series of intellectual freedom documents, which address collection building and user access with broader brush strokes. They include the Policy concerning Confidentiality of Personally Identifiable Information about Library Users; the Policy on Governmental Intimidation; the Resolution on Access to the Use of Libraries and Information by Individuals with Physical or Mental Impairment; Guidelines for the Development and Implementation of Policies, Regulations and Procedures Affecting Access to Library Materials, Services and Facilities; Guidelines for the Development of Policies and Procedures regarding User Behavior and Library Usage; and Dealing with Concerns about Library Resources. As is the case with the policy statements cited above, the *Intellectual Freedom Manual* provides in-depth information regarding the historical background and application of these documents.

A survey of existing library collection development policies indicates that most institutions have either developed their own clearly worded philosophical stance with respect to intellectual freedom or adopted documents promulgated by professional organizations such as the ALA, applicable state library associations, and/or various educational agencies. However, many of these same policies do not include a set of procedural guidelines for handling complaints or other efforts at suppressing library materials and programs. Written (and formally approved) procedures serve as a public relations tool clarifying library actions in addition to ensuring consistent library responses to public complaints.

The *Intellectual Freedom Manual* addresses procedural matters in two sections: "Dealing with Concerns about Library Resources: Procedural Statement" (part II, chapter 8) and "Before the Censor Comes: Essential Preparations" (part III). Three key features—all of which could be integrated into the collection development policy in some manner—are discussed at length in the ALA publication: (1) implementation of an intellectual freedom defense strategy prior to receiving any complaints, (2) reacting to particular censoring attempts, and (3) making available a complaint form to be filled out by the complainant.

The first two points are succinctly covered in "Dealing with Concerns about Library Resources." The complete text of this document reads as follows:

> As with any public service, libraries receive complaints and expressions of concern. One of the librarian's responsibilities is to handle these complaints in a respectful and fair manner. The complaints that librarians often worry about most are those dealing with library resources or free access policies. The key to successfully handling these complaints is to be sure the library staff and governing authorities are all knowledgeable about the complaint procedures and their implementation. As normal operating procedure, each library should:

1. Maintain a materials selection policy. It should be in written form and approved by the appropriate governing authority. It should apply to all library materials equally.
2. Maintain a library service policy. This should cover registration policies, programming, and services in the library that involve access issues.
3. Maintain a clearly defined method for handling complaints. The complaint must be filed in writing and the complainant must be properly identified before action is taken. A decision should be deferred until fully considered by appropriate administrative authority. The process should be followed, whether the complaint originates internally or externally.
4. Maintain in-service training. Conduct periodic in-service training to acquaint staff, administration, and the governing authority with the materials selection policy and library service policy, and procedures for handling complaints.
5. Maintain lines of communication with civic, religious, educational, and political bodies of the community. Library board and staff participation in local civic organizations and presentations to these organizations should emphasize the library's selection process and intellectual freedom principles.
6. Maintain a vigorous public information program on behalf of intellectual freedom. Newspapers, radio, and television should be informed of policies governing resource selection and use, and of any special activities pertaining to intellectual freedom.
7. Maintain familiarity with any local municipal and state legislation pertaining to intellectual freedom and First Amendment rights.[2]

Following these practices will not preclude receiving complaints from pressure groups or individuals but should provide a base from which to operate when these concerns are expressed. When a complaint is made, follow one or more of the steps listed below:

a. Listen calmly and courteously to the complaint. Remember the person has a right to express a concern. Use of good communication skills helps many people understand the need for diversity in library collections and the use of library resources. In the event the person is not satisfied, advise the complainant of the library policy and procedures for handling library resource statements of concern. If a person does fill out a form about their concern, make sure a prompt written reply related to the concern is sent.
b. It is essential to notify the administration and/or the governing authority (library board, etc.) of the complaint and assure them that the library's procedures are being followed. Present full, written information giving the nature of the complaint and identify the source.
c. When appropriate, seek the support of the local media. Freedom to read and freedom of the press go hand in hand.

   d. When appropriate, inform local civic organizations of the facts and enlist their support. Meet negative pressure with positive pressure.

   e. Assert the principles of the Library Bill of Rights as a professional responsibility. Laws governing obscenity, subversive material and other
questionable matter are subject to interpretation by courts. Library materials found to meet the standards set in the materials selection policy
should not be removed from public access until after an adversary hearing resulting in a final judicial determination.

   f. Contact the ALA Office for Intellectual Freedom and your state intellectual freedom committee to inform them of the complaint and enlist
their support and the assistance of other agencies.

The principles and procedures discussed above apply to all kinds of re-
source-related complaints or attempts to censor and are supported by
groups such as the National Education Association, the American Civil
Liberties Union, and the National Council of Teachers of English, as well
as the American Library Association. While the practices provide positive
means for preparing for and meeting pressure group complaints, they serve
the more general purpose of supporting the Library Bill of Rights, particularly Article III, which states, "Libraries should challenge censorship in
the fulfillment of the responsibility to provide information and enlightenment."[3]

The *Intellectual Freedom Manual* also includes a sample complaint form,
titled Request for Reconsideration of Library Resources (revised by the Intellectual Freedom Committee, June 27, 1995). The work recommends that
libraries and librarians consider using it as a model; ALA also encourages
modifications of the form "to reflect the specifics of a given library situation."[4]

A wealth of resource material relating to intellectual freedom is available
on the ALA's Office for Intellectual Freedom website at www.ala.org/
alaorg/oif. Links are arranged under the following headings: Advocates, Documents, Intellectual Freedom in Action, Who We Are and How to Contact Us,
Organizations, References, What You Can Do to Oppose Censorship, and
Mail Comments.

It should be noted that the Library Bill of Rights and all other ALA intellectual freedom documents do not provide any form of legal protection for libraries. These safeguards are limited to the freedom-of-speech provisions
falling within the U.S. Constitution. However, the ALA policy statements
have, in G. Edward Evans's words, "helped librarians recommit themselves
to a philosophy of service based on the premise that users of libraries should
have access to information on all sides of all issues."[5]

Intellectual freedom issues are extremely complex, encompassing a wide range of social, political, legal, religious, and aesthetic considerations. The personal belief systems and professional ethics of library staff are tempered by outside factors such as institutional governance, job security, and community tolerance. The intellectual freedom section of a materials selection policy should be a product of the in-depth thinking and research that is required during the planning stages of a collection-building program.

SAMPLE POLICIES

The samples provided below represent only those portions of each institution's collection development policy directly concerned with intellectual freedom. Peripheral issues (e.g., user access to collections, copyright, media formats falling within the collection's scope) are addressed in other portions of the book. Policies included vary greatly regarding coverage of intellectual freedom issues. For instance, the Apponequet Regional High School Library focuses exclusively on relevant philosophical statements whereas the other institutional policies include a substantial portion concerned with procedures for handling complaints. Differences in physical layout are further influenced by mode of presentation, most notably, traditional print versus Internet home pages (website addresses have been included where applicable). The Northeast Community School District policy illustrates how one particular institution utilizes a Web-based approach with multiple links to the appropriate guidelines. It would appear that these variations reflect the distinctive characteristics and concerns of the institutions combined with the respective visions of library staff. Intellectual freedom statements have been reproduced in Appendix B of this book.

Apponequet Regional High School (Lakeville, Massachusetts) Library

Collection Development and Mission Statements

Policies Adopted The following policies and statements of the American Library Association constitute the foundations of the Library's operating philosophy:

- Library Bill of Rights
- Free Access to Libraries for Minors
- Regulations, Policies, and Procedures Affecting Access to Library Resources and Services

- Statement on Labeling
- Library Access for Children and Young People to Videotapes and Other Nonprint Services
- Expurgation of Library Materials
- Diversity in Collection Development
- Evaluating Library Collections
- Challenged Materials
- Restricted Access to Library Materials
- Library-Initiated Programs as a Resource
- Access to Resources and Services in the School Library Media Program
- The Universal Right to Free Expression
- Dealing with Concerns About Library Resources
- Freedom to Read
- Policy Concerning Confidentiality of Personally Identifiable Information about Library Users

[http://users.rcn.com/libra/mission.html]

Bowling Green (Ohio) City School District

Media Center Materials Selection Policy

Selection of Controversial Materials   Materials on controversial topics, as well as materials containing controversial language, may be included in the Bowling Green City School District Media Centers if they are recommended in the professional and commercial reviewing journals, if they meet the evaluation criteria listed above in this policy, if they are relevant to the curriculum, and are consistent with the Philosophy of Education of our school district.

The Board of Education adopted the following library procedures for dealing with challenged materials:

A. If the first contact is with a secretary or teacher
   1. Try to direct complainant to librarian or principal.
   2. If unwilling to be directed, listen courteously, making no judgments and offering no personal opinions.
B. When contact is with the principal
   1. Listen courteously, making no judgments and offering no personal opinions.
   2. Since no parent or group of parents has the right to determine reading matter for students other than their own, materials shall not be removed from the shelves at this step; however, a parent may request that his child not read a given book, provided written request be made to the principal.

3. If parent is not satisfied with restricting the use of the material with his own child, make an appointment for a three-way conference (complainant, librarian, principal, and/or teacher).
4. Principal will notify the superintendent of the complaint and that "Library Procedures" are being followed.

C. Librarian shall collect reviews and accumulate data on how the material conforms to the selection policy.

D. If at the conclusion of the three-way conference the complainant is still not satisfied, ask him/her to fill out our Complaint Form.

E. Principal shall notify the superintendent and assistant superintendent of the results of the conference. Include copies of complaint form, reviews, and data collected if complaint procedure is continuing.

F. Superintendent shall appoint a review committee to include a librarian, a teacher, an administrator, and a parent. The committee will review the material, judge whether it conforms to the Selection Policy and submit its report in writing to the assistant superintendent, and building principal.

G. If the matter cannot be resolved at the building level, final disposition will be made by the superintendent and the Board of Education. Concerned parties will be notified of the final disposition in writing.

[adopted June 7, 1983; last revision October 2002; http://winslo.state .oh.us/publib/material-bg.html]

Hawaii Department of Education Office of Instructional Services

Materials Selection Policy for School Library Instructional Technology Centers

Challenged Materials   Occasional objections to a selection will be made by the public, despite the care taken to select materials for student and teacher use. In such instances, the principles of the freedom to read and professional responsibility of the staff should be defended.

If a complaint is made, the procedures to follow are:

1. Inform the principal about the situation and, if it seems feasible, set up a conference with complainant, principal, librarian, and any other staff member involved in the complaint. Prior to the conference, consider contacting School Library Services (SLS) for advice on such matters as the following:

   • whether material has been reviewed and rating given the item;
   • whether there are possible sources of local and/or national reviews on material in question; and

- suggestions SLS specialists might have regarding the upcoming conference.

In this initial stage, school staff should try to explain to the complainant:

a. The school's selection procedure, criteria, and qualifications of those
persons selecting the material
b. The particular place the material occupies in the educational program,
its intended educational usefulness, and additional information regarding its use
(Note: The vast majority of complaints can be amicably resolved in the
first stages. A personal conference can often solve the problem where a
shift into a more formal procedure might inflate it.)

2. Should the complainant still not be satisfied, invite the person to file objections in writing and offer to send him or her the Patron Request for
Reevaluation of School Library Media Center Material Form so that
he/she may submit a formal complaint. (See attachment.)
3. Determine whether the material may be sufficiently questionable to warrant its immediate withdrawal pending a decision.
4. Should the situation not be resolved at the school level, the complainant
should be referred to the respective district office.
5. Should the complainant not be satisfied with the District Superintendent's
decision, the matter should be referred to the Assistant Superintendent, Office of Instructional Services. The Assistant Superintendent will refer the
matter to the appropriate specialist for study and recommendations. Specialists will read, examine, and/or reconsider the material in question and report
their findings to the Assistant Superintendent. The Assistant Superintendent
will then respond to the complainant and try to resolve the matter.
6. Should the complainant insist on taking the matter further, the Assistant
Superintendent will then report to the Superintendent who will present
staff recommendations to the Board of Education for a final decision.

[December 1994 revision; last updated September 22, 1999; http://sls.k12
.hi.us/selection.html]

Northeast Community School District (Goose Lake, Iowa)

Instructional Materials Selection

Guidelines for the Treatment of Complaints

COMPLAINTS AND OBJECTIONS   Any resident or employee of the school
district may submit a complaint regarding instructional materials used in the

district's educational program despite the fact that the individuals selecting such material were duly qualified to make the selection, followed the proper procedure, and observed the criteria for selecting such material.

The informal complaint process includes the following steps:

1. The school official or faculty member initially receiving the complaint shall explain to the complainant
   a. the school's selection procedure, criteria, and qualifications of those persons selecting the material; and
   b. the particular place the objected to material occupies in the educational program, its intended educational usefulness, the educational objectives it meets, and any other additional information regarding its use (or refer the complaining party to someone who can identify and explain the use of the material).

   (Comment: The vast majority of complaints can be amicably settled in the first stages when school officials and staff are frequently reminded of the school's procedures. It is highly recommended that both the principal and the faculty member who is using the material or helped select the material meet with the person(s) responsible for the complaint. The person receiving the complaint should at no time agree with the complainant that the material should be removed, but should express appreciation to the person for sharing these concerns. A personal conference may solve the problem where a shift into a more formal procedure might inflate the problem. While the legal right to object to materials is not expressly stated, it is implied in such provisions as the constitutional right to petition the government for redress of grievances.)

2. In the event that the person making an objection to the material is not satisfied with the initial explanation, the person raising the question would be referred to the building principal. If, after private counseling, the complainant desires to file a formal complaint, the principal to whom the complainant has been referred may assist, if the complainant desires help, in filling out a Selection Review Request Form (see Appendix A).

3. The individual receiving the initial complaint shall advise the principal of the attendance center where the challenged material is being used of the initial contact no later than the end of the following school day, whether or not the complainant has apparently been satisfied of the initial contact, and a written record of the contact shall be maintained by the building principal.

4. The Instructional Materials Selection policy shall be reviewed for the staff annually. The staff shall be reminded that the right to object to materials is one granted by policies enacted by the Board of Directors and firmly entrenched in law. Complaints shall be handled with courtesy and integrity.

REQUEST FOR SELECTION REVIEW

1. Any resident or employee of the school district may formally question instructional materials used in the district's educational program on the basis of appropriateness. This procedure is for the purpose of considering the opinions of those persons in the schools and the community who are not directly involved in the selection process.
2. Each attendance center and the school district's central office will keep on hand and make available copies of the Instructional Materials Selection policy and Selection Review Request form. Any formal objections to instructional materials shall be made on this form.
3. The Selection Review Request form shall be signed by the complainant and filed with the Superintendent.
4. Within five business days of the filing of the Form, the Superintendent shall forward it to the Selection Review Committee for reevaluation.
5. Generally, access to challenged materials shall not be restricted during the selection review process. However, in unusual circumstances, the Superintendent may call a special meeting of the committee and the committee could vote to temporarily remove the material. Temporary removal shall require a three-fourths vote of the committee.
6. The Selection Review Committee

    a. The formal Selection Review Committee will be made up of eleven members appointed annually by the Superintendent. It will consist of three teachers (one from each attendance center), one school library/media specialist, one principal, four members of the community (the President of the P.T.O. will select one of them and the Superintendent will select three), and two high school students.
    b. The informal Selection Review Committee shall meet when there are no complaints before the committee. The purpose of these meetings will be to educate committee members about the issues of censorship, intellectual freedom, and freedom of speech. This body will be comprised of fourteen members, including three teachers, two school library/media specialists, three administrators, four community members, and two high school students.

(Comment: A committee with a majority of lay members who are representative of the community should be viewed by the community as being objective and not automatically supportive of prior professional decisions on selection. It is important to establish and maintain the committee's credibility through a majority of nonprofessionals. An appointed committee will generally be more objective than a voluntary committee.)

c. The chairperson and secretary shall be selected at the first committee meeting each year.
d. A calendar of regular meetings shall be established. Notice of regular and special meetings shall be made public through school newsletters and/or calendars.
e. The Selection Review Committee shall receive Selection Review Request Forms from the Superintendent.
f. The procedure for the first meeting following receipt of a Selection Review Request Form will be as follows:
   (1) Distribute copies of written Selection Review Request Form.
   (2) Give complainant or group spokesperson an opportunity to talk about and expand on the Selection Review Request Form.
   (3) Distribute reputable, professionally prepared reviews of the material when available.
   (4) Distribute copies of challenged material as available.
g. At a subsequent meeting, interested persons, including the complainant, may have the opportunity to share their views. The Committee may request that individuals with special knowledge be present to give information to the Committee.
h. The Complainant shall be kept informed by the Secretary concerning the status of his or her complaint throughout the Selection Review process. The Complainant and known interested parties shall be given appropriate notice of such meetings.
i. At the second, or a subsequent meeting, the Committee will deliberate in open session. The Committee's final decision will be to (1) take no removal action, (2) remove all or part of the challenged material from the school environment, or (3) limit the educational use of the challenged material. The sole criterion for the final decision is the appropriateness of the material for its intended educational use. The vote on the decision shall be by secret ballot. The written decision and its justification shall be forwarded to the principals and superintendent, the complainant, other interested persons, and the appropriate attendance centers.
j. A decision to sustain a challenge shall not be interpreted as a judgment of irresponsibility on the part of the professionals involved in the original selection or use of the materials.
k. Requests to review materials which have previously been before the Committee must receive approval of the members before the materials will again be reviewed. Every Selection Review Request Form shall be acted upon by the Committee.
l. Committee members directly associated with the selection, use, or challenge of the material in question shall be excused from the Committee

during the deliberation on such materials. The purpose of this will be to have them serve as a witness to the Committee and to provide information to the Committee. The Superintendent may appoint a temporary replacement for the excused Committee member, but such replacement shall be of the same general qualifications as the person being excused.

(Comment: The Committee should never be placed in the position of appearing to defend itself, its members, or the school staff. The Committee must maintain a non-adversarial position.)

m. If people are not satisfied with the decision of the Selection Review Committee, they may request that the matter be placed on the agenda of the next regularly scheduled meeting of the School Board. These requests should comply with existing School Board policy and rules regarding the School Board agenda. Any district patron, including a district employee, has the implied right to seek a final decision from the Board as the ultimate authority of the district, and have the right to appeal the Board's decision.

n. Any person dissatisfied with the decision of the School Board may appeal to the State Board of Education pursuant to Iowa Code Chapter 290.

[www.iema-ia.org/IEMA106.html]

Rogers (Arkansas) Public School System

District Instructional Materials Selection Policy

Guidelines for Addressing Patron Complaints about Resources   All libraries are pressured from groups and individuals who wish to use the library as an instrument of their own taste. It is the responsibility of every library to take certain measures to clarify policies and establish community relations. They will provide a firm and clearly defined position if selection policies are challenged. As normal operating procedure, each library should consider the following strategies:

1. Maintain a materials selection policy. It should be in written form and approved by the appropriate governing authority. It should apply to all library materials equally.
2. Maintain a clearly defined method for handling complaints. The complaint must be filed in writing and the complainant should be identified before action is taken. A decision should be deferred until fully considered by appropriate administrative authority.

3. Conduct periodic in-service training to acquaint staff, administration, and the governing authority with the materials selection policy and method for handling complaints.
4. Maintain lines of communication with civic, religious, educational and political bodies of the community. Library board and staff participation in local civic organizations and presentations to these organizations should emphasize the library's selection process and intellectual freedom.
5. Maintain familiarity with any local municipal and state legislation pertaining to intellectual freedom and First Amendment rights.

Adherence to these practices will not preclude confrontations with pressure groups or individuals but should provide a base from which to resist efforts to place restraints on the library. If a confrontation does occur, take one or more of the steps listed below:

1. Listen calmly and courteously to the complaint and advise the complainant of the library's procedure for reconsideration of the materials. Don't confuse noise with substance. Handle the complaint according to established rules. Treat the group or individual who complains with dignity and courtesy.
2. Take immediate steps to notify the administration and/or the governing authority (library board, etc.) of the complaint and assure them that the library's procedures are being followed. Present full, written information giving the nature of the complaint and identify the source.
3. When appropriate, seek the support of the local media. Freedom to read and freedom of the press go hand in hand.
4. When appropriate, inform local civic organizations of the facts and enlist their support. Meet negative pressure with positive pressure.
5. Defend the principle of the freedom to read as professional responsibility. Only rarely is it necessary to defend the individual item. Laws governing obscenity, subversive material, and other questionable matter are subject to interpretation of courts. Library materials found to meet the standards set in the selection policy should not be removed from the public access until after an adversary hearing resulting in a final judicial determination.
6. Contact the ALA Office for Intellectual Freedom and your state intellectual freedom committee to inform them of the complaint and to enlist their support in appropriate ways. Even though censorship must be fought at the local level, there is value in the support and assistance of agencies outside the area, which have no personal involvement. They can often cite parallel cases and suggest methods of meeting an attack.

The principles and procedures discussed above apply to all kinds of censorship attacks and are supported by groups such as the National Education Association, the American Civil Liberties Union, and the National Council of Teachers of English, as well as the American Library Association. While the practices provide positive means for preparing for and meeting pressure group complaints, they serve the more general purpose of supporting the Library Bill of Rights, particularly Article 3 which states that "Libraries should challenge censorship in the fulfillment of their responsibility to provide information and enlightenment."

District Challenged Materials Policy

Despite the care taken to select materials for student/teacher use and the qualifications of persons who select the materials, there may be occasional objections. The principles of the freedom to read and the professional responsibility of the staff must be defended.

A. If the complaint is made, the procedures are as follows:

1. Give patron Form A [see table 13.1].
2. Inform all staff members.
3. Upon receipt of written Form A, the Library Council shall designate a Materials Evaluation Committee composed of the following:

- a representative from Central Administrative Staff;
- a representative from building level administration;
- a materials specialist;
- a classroom teacher familiar with the subject challenged;
- a parent; and
- a student, where appropriate.

All members except administrative staff shall be from the school challenged.

B. No material shall be removed from use until the Materials Evaluation Committee has made a final decision.
C. Within 30 days the Materials Evaluation Committee shall

1. examine challenged material in relation to the District Instructional Materials Selection Policy adopted by the Rogers School Board;
2. check general acceptance of the materials by reading reviews;
3. weigh values and faults and form opinion based on the materials as a whole;
4. meet, discuss, and prepare a report to the Library Council (Form B [see table 13.2]); and
5. file a copy of the report with administrative office.

Table 13.1

Form A: Patron's Request for Reconsideration of Work
(Attach extra pages if needed to complete statements)

Author, composer, producer, artist, etc. _____

Title _____

Publisher (if known) _____

Request initiated by _____

Telephone _____ Address _____

Complainant represents: Himself _____ Name of organization _____

Other _____

To what in the work do you object? Please cite specific features: _____

What features of value does the work possess? _____

What do you feel might be the result of reading, viewing, or listening to this work? ____

_____

For what age group is this work appropriate? _____

Did you read, view or listen to the entire work? _____

 If not, what section are you familiar with? _____

Are you aware of the judgment of this work by critics? _____

Are you aware of the teacher's purpose in using this work? _____

What do you believe is the theme or purpose of this work? _____

What would you prefer the school do about this work?

_____ Do not assign or recommend it to my child.

_____ Withdraw it from all students.

_____ Send it back to the proper department grade level for reevaluation.

In its place, what work of equal value would you recommend that would convey as valuable a picture and perspective of a society or set of values?

Signature of Complainant _____ Date _____

Table 13.2

Form B: Materials Evaluation Committee Report
(Attach extra pages if needed to complete statements)

Physical description of challenged material (author, title, publisher, copyright, producer, etc.): _____

Justification for inclusion of material (include theme and purpose): _____

Critical judgment of material (if possible, include copies of reviews indicating the source): _____

Material Evaluation Committee's decision and comments (include statements from majority and minority positions): _____

Copies sent to (signatures of committee members and complainant):

_____

_____

_____

D. If documentation is sufficient, an appeal to the school board may be warranted. Decision of the school board is final.

[www.rogers.k12.ar.us/users/mcook/selection.html]

NOTES

1. American Association of School Librarians and Association for Communications and Technology, eds., *Intellectual Freedom Manual*, 5th ed. (Chicago: ALA Office for Intellectual Freedom, 1996), 207.
2. American Association of School Librarians and Association for Communications and Technology, eds., *Intellectual Freedom Manual*, 187–189.
3. American Association of School Librarians and Association for Communications and Technology, eds., *Intellectual Freedom Manual*, 209–217.
4. American Association of School Librarians and Association for Communications and Technology, eds., *Intellectual Freedom Manual*, 210.
5. G. Edward Evans, *Developing Library Collections* (Englewood, CO: Libraries Unlimited, 1972), 302.

Chapter Fourteen

Copyright

Although directly applicable to collection building and the dissemination of information, copyright and other intellectual property concerns are rarely addressed in written policies. Probable reasons for this include the absence of legal precedents to assist in interpreting specific copyright applications as well as school librarians' general lack of knowledge regarding such issues.

Those policies that do mention copyright tend to focus on the institution's commitment to following legal directives. Other possible concerns to be addressed within a copyright policy include

- discussion of individual library activities and services involving some form of copyright compliance (e.g., photo duplication, interlibrary loan, document delivery, public presentations, licensing of computer software);
- reference to key documents guiding copyright-related decisions such as sections 107 and 108 of the 1976 Copyright Act, the Digital Millennium Copyright Act (1998), the Copyright Term Extension Act (1998), and notable federal court decision and committee guidelines (e.g., Guidelines for Classroom Copying in Not-for-Profit Educational Institutions); and
- procedures for educating the library's staff and constituency (e.g., posting guidelines near copy machines).

The incorporation of copyright information in collection development policies is likely to increase as schools—and, more specifically, instructional media centers—become more committed to digital technologies and are therefore forced to address property rights relating to the storage, manipulation, and transfer of electronic information. Legal advisers are insisting that school media specialists keep relevant copyright statutes close at hand, if not actually citing them in collection policies or, better still, reproducing the text of the documents in the appendixes. By making copyright statements available in this manner, library staff can enhance the execution of their primary mission—educating the student body.

SAMPLE POLICIES

Aldine Independent School District (Houston, Texas) Library Media Services Department

Policy and Procedures Manual

Copyright The library media specialist has the obligation of being informed of copyright laws that affect students and staff and their use of library materials. "To that end, it is worthwhile for the library media specialist to establish and maintain clear and thorough copyright records, and to inform patrons of their obligation under the copyright law." (Simpson 1994, 13) Therefore, in the library, the following books should be in the Professional section:

Bruweleide, Janis H. *The Copyright Primer for Librarians and Educators.* 2nd edition. American Library Association, 1995.
Simpson, Carol Mann. *Copyright for School Libraries: A Practical Guide.* Linworth Publishing, 1994.

[revised June 1999; www.aldine.k12.tx.us]

Norman (Oklahoma) Public Schools Library

Media Program Procedure Manual

Reproduction of Copyrighted Materials It is the intent of the Board to delineate, enforce and abide by the provisions of current copyright laws as they affect the District and its employees.

Copyrighted materials, whether they are print or nonprint, will not be duplicated unless such reproduction meets "fair use" standards or unless written permission from the copyright holder has been received.

Details about "fair use" (that copying which is allowed by federal law) will be made available to all teachers. A summary of these standards will be posted or otherwise made easily available at each machine used for making copies.

The Board does not sanction illegal duplication in any form. Employees who willfully disregard the district's copyright position are in violation of Board Policy; they do so at their own risk and assume all liability responsibility.

[adopted August 8, 1988; staff.norman.k12.ok.us/~klewis/Handbook/copyright policy.html]

Northeast Community School District (Goose Lake, Iowa)

Instructional Materials Selection (Policy)

Copyright Law   The Northeast Community School District will obey the Copyright Act of 1976 and the guidelines for fair use. The purpose of the law is to promote the creation and dissemination of knowledge and ideas and to insure that authors, artists, etc., receive reasonable reward for their efforts. Educators may copy materials following these guidelines:

1. The decision must be spontaneous, occurring so close to intended time of classroom use that permission can't be obtained.
2. The reproduced item must be short in length and/or a relatively small portion of the overall work; i.e., a single copy of a book chapter, article, short story, essay, poem (less than 250 words), map, etc.
3. The cumulative effect of the copying must not entail more than three items from the same source at one time or more than nine instances per semester.
4. Copied materials cannot be employed in anthologies, compilations, or collective works.

For more complete information, see Virginia Helm's *What Educators Should Know About Copyright*, Phi Delta Kappa Educational Foundation, 1986, 50 p. (This source is available in the High School Library, call number 341.7 Helm.) [revised March 25, 1990; January 3, 1995; October 25, 1995; www.iema-ia.org/IEMA101.html]

Chapter Fifteen

Collection Maintenance

Collection maintenance—which includes binding, disaster preparedness, preservation, replacement, and weeding—has received increased attention in recent years. This can be attributed largely to advances in knowledge regarding media care and renewed emphasis on protecting library resources in the face of exploding costs for both new technology and traditional materials. Many large public and academic libraries have utilized binding procedures, disaster plans, preservation programs, and the like for some time, although they are rarely included in collection development statements. Lacking the financial resources and archival imperatives of these institutions, collection maintenance has received comparatively little attention on the part of school media specialists. When addressed in school policies, maintenance issues—for example, binding, inventory procedures—rarely stray far from hardcore weeding concerns.

Perhaps due to concerns regarding stylistic flow, some libraries have chosen to cover such topics within the appendixes rather than as part of the text. Institutions opting to keep such documentation separate from the written policy altogether would be advised to note its existence somewhere within the text. In such cases, the cited documents should be readily accessible if requested by staff, administrators, or clientele.

SAMPLE POLICIES

Many libraries incorporate their weeding policies into the overall collection maintenance portion of the policy. The sample policy excerpts included below are largely concerned with other aspects of collection maintenance, whereas statements exclusively concerned with weeding are located in the that chapter.

Baltimore County (Towson, Maryland) Public Schools

Selection Criteria for School Library Media Center Collections

Assessment and Inventory Process An essential step in collection development is assessment of the needs of the curriculum and student population
with regard to library media resources. Library media specialists will develop
yearly and long-range plans to assist in ongoing assessment. Assessment of
the collection includes taking inventory of existing materials, assessing materials in relation to needs of instructional units, and weeding outdated and inappropriate materials.

The inventory is a process by which holdings are checked against the automated cataloging system and the actual item to determine if the resource is still
part of the collection and still meets selection criteria. The objective of this inventory is to ensure that the automated cataloging system accurately reflects the
collection, which is the key access point for students and teachers to locate information within the library. This procedure should not disrupt the library media
program as automation of school library holdings greatly speed up the process
using the barcode scanning feature. An annual inventory is recommended as the
data is critical to making collection development decisions about the quality and
quantity of the collection in meeting the needs of students and staff.

Inventory Procedures
WEEDING LIBRARY MEDIA MATERIALS A good collection development
plan must include weeding. The process of weeding is a key part of assessing
the collection. It helps keep collections relevant, accurate, and useful; and it
facilitates more effective use of space in the library media center.

Library media materials should be weeded if they

- are in poor physical condition;
- have not been circulated in the last five years;
- are outdated in content, use, or accuracy (copyright date should be considered, but not function as the sole determinant for weeding; some older material may be considered classic or possess considerable historical value to
  the collection);
- are mediocre or poor in quality;
- are biased or portray stereotypes;
- are inappropriate in reading level;
- duplicate information, which is no longer in heavy demand;
- are superseded by new or revised information;
- are outdated with an unattractive format, design, graphics, and illustrations;
- contain information, which is inaccessible because they lack a table of contents, adequate indexing, and searching capabilities; or
- are not selected in accordance with general selection criteria.

WITHDRAWING LIBRARY MEDIA MATERIALS   Although the final decision to withdraw materials from the library media collection is one which is made by the library media specialist, subject area, grade level teachers, and other faculty members may be invited to review the items marked for withdrawal. All withdrawn materials must be sent to classrooms; the same standard of quality applies to all other instructional materials within the school.

REBINDING PROCEDURES   Some books can be easily repaired by the library media specialist. If a book cannot be repaired locally, a decision must be made to rebind or reorder the book.

Rebinding is usually not an attractive or cost efficient option. Books that are rebound will have plain cloth covers without printed titles, illustrations, or book jackets. The best candidates for rebinding are expensive reference books and textbooks which are updated and expected to stay in the collection. Out of print books should be carefully evaluated as to their merit before rebinding. Books which have dirty, torn, or brittle pages should be reordered and not sent for rebinding.

The cost of rebinding will be billed to the local school library. The total expenditure must be deducted from the next year's library materials allotment. Although the cost of rebinding varies yearly according to the bid price, an average book can be estimated at 25% of the replacement cost. The *Rebound Book* form is issued annually in late spring along with updated price list and instructions. Follow these procedures for books that need rebinding:

- Be sure that books meet the minimum binding requirements of 1/2" to 1" inside margin for optimum readability.
- Remove circulation cards from books.
- Update Library Pro Automation software to provide a record of books sent for rebinding.
- Box books for pickup in accordance with rebinding BCPS instructions.
- Deduct the actual expenditure.

[www.bcps.org/offices/lis/office/admin/selection.html]

Longview (Texas) Independent School District

Handbook of Policies and Procedures for Library Services K–12

Maintenance of Library Media and Equipment
DAILY INSPECTION OF LIBRARY MEDIA BEFORE RETURNING TO SHELVES
One of the daily routines in the library is the inspection of library media as they are checked in. Damaged items need to be put aside until repairs can be affected. Daily inspection will insure that the correct person be charged for any damage

that might have occurred (see Payment for Damaged Books section) and that library media are ready for circulation again. Some librarians choose to make pencil notes on front flyleaf regarding damages. Set aside the following:

- Books with torn or loose pages
- Any item with marked pages
- Books with loose bindings
- Any item with torn or loose plastic covers
- Other damaged items needing mending or possible withdrawal from circulation

BOOKS TO BE MENDED

1. Books need mending when any book pages are loose, torn, or rumpled and when the spine is breaking at the joints. If the book is too damaged to circulate, place it on a shelf for books to be sent to the bindery.
2. Avoid extensive mending of a book that is to be rebound.

MINOR REPAIR OF AUDIOVISUAL EQUIPMENT

1. The librarian or assigned person in each school is responsible for performing minor maintenance tasks such as replacement of projection lamps, exciter lamps, and fuses.
2. Preventive maintenance prolongs the life of equipment:
   a. All libraries should have an audiovisual equipment maintenance kit. It should contain lint-free cloths and alcohol to clean lenses and glass. Screwdrivers, pliers, assorted screws, and a hammer are included for minor repair of audiovisual equipment.
   b. Replacement bulbs are sensitive to skin oils and should always be handled with a cloth.
   c. Teachers and students need instruction in the use of various types of equipment.

MAJOR REPAIR OF AUDIOVISUAL EQUIPMENT   Instruction will be given at the beginning of each school year as to whether campus librarian should directly contact equipment repairman, or instead, contact Library Supervisor. Library staff members should complete the LISD Equipment Repair Form in accordance with instructions in the Handbook under "LISD Forms." If any piece of equipment leaves the campus, it is essential that the librarian has a record of the item (including serial number), date out for repair, and name of repairman. Campus librarian is responsible for follow-up regarding return of items.

REBINDING   Careful inspection is made and consideration given to the book's value before rebinding is done. A book is ready to be rebound when the thread with which it is sewn loosens sufficiently that pages fall out, or when its backing cloth is broken, or when its cover is ragged and frayed. Books which receive hard, continuous use and have established value are usually selected for rebinding.

The following types of books are not to be rebound:

1. Books with inner margins less than one inch in width
2. Books with missing pages
3. Books that are out of date
4. Books with fine print or brittle paper
5. Textbooks
6. Books unsuitable for the particular educational level of the school

Guidelines in preparing books for shipment to the bindery:

1. See that the mark of ownership and call number are on the title page of each book.
2. "Check out" book to the bindery.
3. Tie together any book so badly broken that it might fall apart.
4. Tie together any set of books requiring uniform binding.
5. Prepare a list of books to be rebound, arranged alphabetically by author. Retain one copy of the list for library files and send one copy to the Library Supervisor.
6. Pack the books in strong boxes and mark plainly, "Books to be rebound, _____ School."
7. Send the books to the IRC during the final week of school.

DISCARDING   In discarding, use the following guidelines from the Texas State Library Crew Manual:

"MUSTY" is an easily remembered acronym for five negative factors, which frequently ruin a book's usefulness and mark it for weeding.
M = Misleading (and/or factually inaccurate)
U = Ugly (worn and beyond mending or rebinding)
S = Superceded (by a truly new edition or by a much better book on the subject)
T = Trivial (of no discernible literary or scientific merit)
Y = Your collection has no use for this book (irrelevant to the needs and interest of your community)

Use the Crew Manual formulas in weeding the book collection.

Responsibility for Decision to Discard: The librarian has the responsibility for deciding which materials to discard. Contact the Library Supervisor after books have been pulled, but before disposal.

Procedure for Disposal

1. Remove the barcode, spine label, pocket, and card from each book. Make a note to later delete from database. Don't delete until you have made a list of discarded books to keep with final inventory information for the year. You must delete copy record first, then MARC record if there are no other copies.
2. Remove the cover of the book and any worthwhile illustrations or sections.
3. Write or stamp a mark of withdrawal on the face of each book. This includes the name of the school and the date.
4. Dispose of the remaining contents either by giving them to teachers, putting them in the school's paper drive, or in the garbage disposal if totally unusable.
5. Mark "withdrawn" and record the date, opposite the copy entry on the shelf-list records (if campus has shelf list). Delete from database as described in #2 above.
6. If it is the only or last copy of the book, remove the shelf-list card from the file and remove all catalog cards from the card catalog.
7. File the shelf-list card and all catalog cards alphabetically by sets in the withdrawal file. Discard catalog cards after one year. Retain shelf-list card for ten years.

INVENTORY

A. Inventory—Books

The following is suggested as a general procedure. The campus librarian may develop one that is somewhat different if the same end is achieved. Any procedures that differ should be documented. With the Follett program, the inventory does not actually have to be performed either at the end of the year or at one time. These steps do, however, make the procedure somewhat more logical for the librarian.
1. Call in all books in sections to be inventoried.
2. Arrange books in correct order on the shelves as much as possible:
   a. Fiction—Alphabetically by author, then alphabetically by title when there are additional titles by the same author.
   b. Easy Books—Same as fiction.
   c. Nonfiction—Numerically by call number and alphabetically by author within each number.

3. Follow Follett procedures for beginning a new inventory, etc.
4. Using PhD or computer scanner, scan books. Record order of scans so that you will know which areas are complete. Periodically check for unmarked books and compare to shelves, in the event that some books were missed. Shortly before finalizing the inventory, print list of "missing" materials. These are items that were missing from the previous inventory. Determine whether these are still missing. If so, delete items from the database, first by barcode and then, if appropriate, by MARC record. Retain printed list with the note "these deleted from database (date)" with inventory records.
5. Remove shelf-list cards, or note missing copies on cards. Make a note as to whether catalog cards have or have not been pulled.
6. Remove the catalog cards, including all subject heading and analytical cards, for titles that are not to be replaced. If this can be done during inventory time, do so. It may be necessary to hold this activity until the following year. Just be sure cards are labeled as in #5.
7. File the shelf-list card and all catalog cards alphabetically by sets in a withdrawal file for a period of one year. After one year, keep shelf-list but discard the catalog cards. On each shelf-list card, make a pencil note "cat cds pulled" in top margin so that it is obvious that catalog cards have been pulled.
8. Inventory count is to reflect whatever is still in the Follett database.
9. Complete the School Library Inventory (Form L-04) and submit to the Library Supervisor by June 1, or before you leave for the summer.

B. Inventory—Audiovisual Materials
1. An annual inventory of school's audiovisual media collection is required (Form L-05). If any or all media is on the Follett database, attach a Follett report.
2. The library staff records withdrawals on the shelf-list or on a separate database and, where applicable, follows the procedure outlined in the book inventory.

C. Inventory—Audiovisual Equipment
1. Complete the School Inventory of AV Equipment (Form L-07) to submit to the Library Supervisor each spring (the date will be announced annually at district library meetings). Completion of this form will produce a central record of all audiovisual equipment on each campus. The Master Heading List (Form L-06) is used to determine the terminology for each type of equipment. Equipment from all funding sources (not only capital allotments, chapter or title funds, PTA, etc.) is listed. Specific instructions for the completion of Form L-07 are given in the "Library Forms" section of this Handbook. One copy of

this report is retained in the campus library, one copy is given to the campus principal, and one copy is submitted to the Library Supervisor.

2. Check the "Inventory by Campus Room" printout for the library. This printout comes to the principal from the Business Office each spring, usually in April. Equipment is listed here by purchase data, so there is no grouping of like equipment. Librarians should refer to the previously completed Form L-07, rather than checking equipment again at this time. The items listed on this printout include only those purchased with local funds. There will thus be items on the Form L-07 that are not included on the printout.

3. Obsolete equipment, equipment with frequent repair records, or any equipment no longer in use is a candidate for removal from the school's inventory. The campus librarian should first contact the Library Supervisor in the event that equipment could be used at another location. Discarded equipment is so noted on both inventory forms described above.

[1997–1998 edition; 1301 E. Young Street, Longview, TX 75602]

Chapter Sixteen

Weeding

Weeding—sometimes referred to as deselection or negative selection by library professionals—has traditionally been one of the most overlooked components of the collection management process. For a variety of reasons—most notably, time limitations, the tendency to place a higher priority on other activities (particularly within the school environment), a personal distaste for disposing of books and other information sources, and the fear of offending patrons and administrators—cause librarians to avoid (or at least put off) this function. Therefore, it is essential that collection developers have access to written weeding guidelines.

Above all, the weeding section should emphasize policy rather than procedures. Rose Mary Magrill and John Corbin address the differences between these two concepts in their work *Acquisition Management and Collection Development in Libraries*:

> The ideal . . . policy clearly indicates the general intent of the library administration with regard to the collection and is both generally applicable and adequately flexible. Policies are sometimes confused with procedures, which are entirely different. A procedure statement documents the best way to carry out a specific activity, giving detailed, step-by-step instructions. While procedures leave little room for individual judgment, policies spell out limits of acceptable action and grant freedom to exercise professional judgment within those limits.[1]

From this perspective, an effective weeding document sets forth a philosophical stance based on the library's mission and goals as well as documented client needs. Although many libraries include various procedures within the collection development policy, there appears to be widespread agreement that the weeding statement should be much more than a listing of steps or directives. Some institutions, in fact, include weeding procedures in a separate document utilized primarily by library staff. In such cases, a copy of these procedures—in addition to any other guidelines dictating collection-building practices—should be retained in a readily accessible place, particularly when cited in the policy.

Libraries lacking useful weeding procedures can consult a wide array of professional sources such as *The CREW Method: Expanded Guidelines for Collection Evaluation and Weeding for Small and Medium-Sized Libraries* (1995), published by the Texas State Library and Archives Commission. Vital procedures should include checking the circulation record of an item in order to determine how often and how recently it has been used, noting copyright dates for currency in subject areas where this is an issue, consulting tables of contents or indexes for relevance, checking statements of fact for accuracy, assessing physical condition, and ascertaining whether other materials on the subject are available in the holdings. Procedures often include directions for the consideration of special formats.

Providing a rationale for weeding that itemizes the advantages associated with the process should prove useful in securing staff support while neutralizing outside criticism. Both school librarians and library users would generally agree that comprehensive collection building is not feasible due to limitations in space and resources. Once this fact has been acknowledged, it is imperative to construct an effective decision-making model for weeding.

Content criteria guidelines constitute the core of a weeding policy. These guidelines will mirror to a considerable extent the evaluation criteria outlined in the selection process. Therefore, to achieve the best results, librarians involved in selection should also be responsible for weeding. Acknowledging that specificity can be important to understanding, weeding criteria should nevertheless be general enough to provide librarians some degree of latitude in the decision-making process.

A structured periodic review process is essential to the weeding process and should be documented in writing. For libraries possessing limited slow periods (work days immediately before or after the academic year are widely employed by school librarians), the weeding schedule must be adapted to the daily routine. The key is not to approach the process as an unimportant last-minute addition to the overall collection-building plan.

The weeding policy should also consider options to outright discarding, whereby references to the material are removed from library records and the material itself is destroyed. These alternatives include

• relegation, in which the material is removed from the open shelves, or from easy access, and stored in stacks, or at some remote location;

- transference of the material to group storage, in which case there could be common ownership (perhaps at the district level) of the material and access to it, or else the library could retain ownership, even though there might be some form of common storage; and
- transference of the ownership, in which case access could be possible if the material is transferred to another library, but difficult or impossible if it is transferred to private ownership, by sale to the public.[2]

SAMPLE POLICIES

The following policy excerpts reflect the various approaches to weeding employed by libraries. They also illustrate the issues (e.g., evaluative criteria, procedures) of greatest concern to these institutions.

Squires Elementary School (Fayette County, Kentucky) Library

Collection Development & Material Selection Policy

Weeding the Library Collection   Weeding should entail the same care, thought and judgment as selection. Thought should be on the goals of the library as well as the availability of funds for replacement of existing titles before older materials which are still useful for the collection are weeded.

Why weed? It provides a more appealing, more up-to-date collection, makes the media center easier to use, ensures a reputation for providing reliable information, provides feedback on the strengths and weaknesses of the collection, facilitates identification of works which need repair or replacement, and makes space. In other words, it provides a means to enhance the credibility and use of the collection.

In general, last copies and out-of-print books are retained, if their informational value is secure (i.e., not out-of-date and harmful to the community). Once the library is at maximum count, one book should be weeded for every one acquired.

Books that should be weeded from the collection include the following:

- Duplicate copies of titles that are no longer in demand; three to five years without circulating and librarians' knowledge that it has not been used in the library for reference would probably warrant discarding
- Titles, which have been superseded by newer editions
- Books that are worn, damaged, or not in sufficient demand to justify extensive repair or rebinding

- Books that contain out-of-date material and which are superseded by more current titles in any given category
- Sets of textbooks and old textbooks unless single copies are to be used for reference
- Sets of readers, which can be returned to the classroom or other storage areas

Generally, Segal's MUSTY is used for weeding:

- M = Misleading (and/or factually inaccurate)
- U = Ugly (condition beyond mending, rebinding or repairing)
- S = Superseded (by a truly new edition or by a much better item on the subject)
- T = Trivial (of no discernible literary or scientific merit)
- Y = Your collection has no use for this item

Commonly accepted practices include considering the age of the item and the last date it circulated.

Weeded books that are damaged beyond repair are destroyed. Those others are labeled DISCARD with black marker on the inside cover and are sent to Media Services.

Materials the library will keep include the classics, unless a more attractive format is available; local and state history materials, unless they can be replaced with new copies; annuals and other major publications of the school; archival materials, such as public relations brochures and bond advertising, if not maintained by another unit of the schools; and items incorrectly classified or poorly promoted, which might be circulated under changed circumstances.

GUIDELINES IN WEEDING NONFICTION

000	Encyclopedias	New edition is needed at least every five years.
	Bibliographies	Seldom of use after five years from day of copyright.
	Guides/Literature	Value determined by use.
100	Philosophy, Ethics	Value determined by use. Less scholarly works are useless after ten years.
200	Religion	Value determined by use. Collection should contain basic information (but not propaganda) about as many sects and religions as possible.
300	Social Sciences	Controversial issues should be well represented from all sides.

	Almanacs/Yrbks.	Superseded by each new volume. Seldom of much use after five years.
320	Politics, Economics	Books dealing with historical aspects determined by use. Discard timely or topical material after approximately ten years. Replace with new editions when available.
340/50	Government	Ten years; new titles supersede older materials.
360	Social welfare	Weeding depends on use. Most non-historical materials are passed after ten years.
370/80	Educ./Commerce	Keep historical materials if they are likely to be used. Non-historical materials should be replaced within ten years.
390	Folkways	Keep basic material; weeding depends on use.
400	Languages	Keep basic material; weeding depends on use.
500	Pure science	Typically out-of-date within five years; exceptions are botany and natural history.
600/18	Invention, Medicine	Five-year limit; exceptions are basic material on inventions and anatomy.
620	Animal husbandry	Keep up-to-date as new editions and new material become available.
621	Radio, Television	Five-year limit, except for historical material.
630	Farming, etc.	Keep up-to-date as new editions and new material become available.
640	Home economics	Weeding depends on use. Emphasize currency; exception: keep all cookbooks.
650	Business, etc.	Ten-year limit.
	Chem./ Food products	Five to ten-year limit, based on content.
690	Manuf./Building	Ten-year limit; exception: older materials on crafts, clocks, guns, and toys may be useful.
700	Art, Music	Retain basic material.
800	Literature	Retain basic material.
900	History	Depends on community use and needs, factual accuracy, and objectivity.
910	Travel, Geography	Travel books published before 1960 discarded unless of value from historical standpoint or as personal account.

	Pre-1970 African, European, and Asiatic geography only of historical interest. Titles marred by misinformation should be discarded.
Biography	Unless subject has permanent interest or importance, weed as soon as demand subsides. Replace biographies with mediocre literary value as better options appear. Retain titles that are outstanding in content or style if still useful.
Rare Books	List books published prior to 1900 and other old editions possessing potential value, and send to State Library or nearby research institution for advice regarding value, possible sale to rare book dealer, or storage in appropriate libraries.
Serials	Retain five years if in demand for reference. Magazines may be kept longer, and bound after one year. With limited space, bound volumes may be disposed of after ten years. Microforms should always be a viable option.
Pamphlets	Weed according to general nonfiction guidelines; retain only up-to-date materials.
Govt. documents	Order and discard based on use and requests of patrons.

[www.squires.fayette.k12.ky.us/library/collect.htm]

University Laboratory High School (Urbana, Illinois) Library

Collection Development Policy

Weeding

A. PURPOSE The University Laboratory High School Library recognizes the importance of maintaining a collection of current, appropriate, and useful materials. Therefore, a periodic evaluation of the collection will be performed in order to remove or replace materials, which are no longer useful. The following guidelines have been developed to aid in the weeding process; however, the final decision concerning the removal or replacement of material rests with the University Laboratory High School librarian.

B. GUIDELINES

1. Weeding by Appearance
   - Worn-out volumes: dirty, brittle, yellow pages; missing pages; tattered covers; etc.
   - Badly bound volumes: soft, pulpy paper and/or shoddy binding
   - Badly printed works
   - Books of antiquated appearance which might discourage use
   - Audio-visual materials with missing or broken pieces
2. Weeding of Superfluous or Duplicate Volumes
   - Unneeded duplicate titles
   - Older editions
   - Highly specialized books (when library holds more general or up-to-date volumes on the same subject)
   - Books on subjects of little interest to the local community
   - Books which no longer relate to the curriculum (if specialized)
3. Weeding Based on Poor Content
   - Information is dated
   - Information is inaccurate
   - Stereotypes are present
   - Book is poorly written
4. Weeding According to Use
   - Nonfiction: Book has not been checked out within last 10 years
   - Fiction: Book has not been checked out within last 5 years (classics excluded)

Categories of books that may be quickly outdated:

- 000s: computers
- 100s: psychology (especially popular literature)
- 300s: college & career materials
- 400s: grammars with dated examples and/or illustrations
- 500s: astronomy, chemistry, physics, biology
- 600s: electronics, engineering, health, technology
- 900s: popular biographies
- mistakes in selection/acquisition

Categories of books that are not quickly outdated:

- dictionaries
- biographical sources

- literary criticism
- classics of literature
- foreign language literature
- art books
- local history/geography
- books providing general principles of a subject or discipline

[revised February 2000; last modified July 2001; www.uni.uiuc.edu/library/policies/collectiondevelopment.html]

Wilmington (Vermont) School District

Collection Development Policy

Maintenance/Weeding Maintenance of the collection is an ongoing process. Materials and information resources will continually be evaluated in regard to their contribution to the collection as a whole and in the relationship to their physical condition and usefulness to the specific population served. The goal of the maintenance policy is to preserve the integrity of the collection. In order to maintain quality, increase efficiency, improve reliability, increase use and usefulness, and relieve crowding, materials that no longer meet the school's selection criteria, are obsolete or beyond use, must be removed or weeded from the collection. The ultimate decision for weeding materials from the collection is the responsibility of the school library media specialist. [www.dves.k12.vt.us/Users/cethier/libpol.html]

NOTES

1. Rose Mary Magrill and John Corbin, *Acquisition Management and Collection Development in Libraries*, 2nd ed. (Chicago: American Library Association, 1989), 29.

2. G. E. Gorman and B. R. Howes, *Collection Development for Libraries* (London: Bowker-Saur, 1990), 324–25.

Seventeen

Collection Evaluation

The evaluation of library holdings is currently recognized as one of the most important collection management functions.[1] This process, while hardly a recent development, has gained importance due to general reduction of acquisition budgets beginning in the 1980s and the expansion of cooperative planning among libraries.[2] In a seminal article published in the January 1974 issue of *Library Trends*, George Bonn identified five distinct methods of evaluating library collections:

1. Compiling statistics on holdings, use, and expenditures
2. Checking lists, catalogs, and bibliographies
3. Obtaining opinions from regular users
4. Examining the collection directly
5. Applying standards, plus testing the library's document delivery capability and noting the relative use of several libraries by a particular group[3]

All of these techniques remain useful to the present day, although it could be argued that a combination of two or more types provide a greater likelihood of obtaining an accurate indicator of collection strength. Faced with the considerable time and resource (staff, funding) demands typifying a collection assessment program, a number of scaled-down methodologies have appeared in the literature in recent years, most of which claim to sacrifice little in the way of reliability.[4]

It is imperative that libraries of all types implement a sound collection assessment strategy as a precondition for achieving service excellence. Given the wide array of options available, the collection development policy's evaluation section serves to delineate the process adopted by the library.

SAMPLE POLICIES

While the Baltimore County Public Schools and Wilmington School District libraries both appear to actively practice collection assessment, they take divergent paths in documenting this commitment. The Baltimore County system seems to utilize the first three methods of the Bonn typology, that is, compiling data regarding library holdings and determining the effectiveness of the collection in meeting curricular needs. Although the techniques utilized to accomplish the latter objectives are not discussed in the policy, it seems likely that they include the use of key selection tools and soliciting clientele feedback. On the other hand, the Wilmington School District focuses on Bonn's fourth and fifth points, direct examination of the collection via inventory and recourse to regional accreditation standards.

Baltimore County (Towson, Maryland) Public Schools

Selection Policy for School Library Media Center Collections

Assessment of the Library Media Collection   Collection assessment is needed to determine the quality of the existing library media collection. It is an organized method for collecting statistics on the age of the collection, the number of titles in the collection, and the ability of the collection to meet curricular needs. [www.bcps.org/offices/lis/office/admin/selection.html]

Wilmington (Vermont) School District

Collection Development Policy

Evaluation   Both the Deerfield Valley Elementary School and the Wilmington Middle/Senior High School use the Library Media Evaluation/Indicators as a tool for evaluating the library program. The document, on file in each library, addresses four areas which are necessary for student success: access, use, collaboration, and professional development.

The breadth and depth of the collection at the Wilmington Middle/Senior High School media center will be measured also during the evaluation process of the New England Association of Schools and Colleges. A thorough inventory will be taken at the end of each school year. [www.dves.k12.vt.us/Users/cethier/libpol.html]

NOTES

1. Michael R. Gabriel, *Collection Development and Collection Evaluation: A Sourcebook* (Metuchen, NJ: Scarecrow, 1995), 77.

2. Eugene Wiemers, et al. "Collection Evaluation: A Practical Guide to the Literature," *Library Acquisitions Practice and Theory* 8, no. 1 (1984): 65–78.

3. George Bonn, "Evaluation of the Collection," *Library Trends* 22 (January 1974): 265–304.

4. Among the collection assessment tools developed in recent years, those outlined in the following sources place a premium on the minimal expenditure of time and resources: David V. Loertscher, "Collection Mapping—An Evaluation Strategy for Collection Development," *Drexel Library Quarterly* (Spring 1985): 9–39; M. D. Lopez, "Lopez or Citation Technique of In-Depth Collection Evaluation Explicated," *College and Research Libraries* (May 1983): 251–55; M. Sandler, "Quantitative Approaches to Qualitative Collection Assessment," *Collection Building* 4 (1987): 12–17; Howard D. White, *Brief Tests of Collection Strength: A Methodology for All Types of Libraries* (Westport, CT: Greenwood, 1995).

Chapter Eighteen

Services/Special Features

Although not directly concerned with collection building functions (e.g., the evaluation of materials, weeding), many library services influence the character of library holdings. Collection development statements generally omit descriptions of these services. However, some institutions choose to include either a general inventory of services or describe in greater detail those programs placing noteworthy demands on library holdings. An increasing number of libraries are posting their policies on institutional websites along with hyperlinks to sections describing organizational services. While it might be argued that these service statements were not envisioned as part of the core written policy, the very presence of hyperlinks makes clear the intended connection.

SAMPLE POLICIES

The policy excerpts below reflect two divergent approaches for discussing library services within the context of collection building. The Longview Independent School District outlines its overriding objectives for media center services in addition to addressing library instruction in greater detail. In contrast, the Aldine Independent School District delineates two of its most prestigious reading programs.

Aldine Independent School District (Houston, Texas) Library Media Services Department

Policy and Procedures Manual

Reading Programs

TEXAS BLUEBONNET AWARD   Administration—The Texas Bluebonnet Award, a project of the Texas Library Association (TLA), is sponsored by the Texas Association of School Librarians and the Children's Round Table for students in grades 3–6. An annual list of twenty books is selected by the Texas Bluebonnet Award Committee.

Purpose—The Texas Bluebonnet Award is designed to encouraged Texas children grades 3–6 to read more books, to explore a variety of current literature, to develop powers of discrimination, and to identify their favorite books through the voting process.

Participation—Schools participating in the TBA program pay an annual registration fee of $5.00 per library. The registration year is from April 1 to March 31. Students in grades 3–6 are encouraged to read books from an annual master list of twenty titles. Those children who read (or hear read aloud) five or more books on the master list are eligible to vote in January for their favorite title. The author of the book voted the favorite in a statewide vote is honored with a medallion presented at the TLA annual conference usually held in April. Ten children who participated in the reading and voting are selected by a random drawing to present the author's award.

Registration—Registration information is routinely mailed to schools but registration forms may be accessed through the TLA–Texas Bluebonnet Award website (http://txla.org/html/tba_info.html). An annual registration fee of $5.00 for each participating school library should be submitted by the librarian. The registration period extends from April 1 through March 31 of the next calendar year. Registration should be sent to Texas Bluebonnet Award, Texas Library Association, 3355 Bee Cave Road, Suite 401, Austin, TX 78746-6763. A master reading list and various enrichment suggestions are mailed to each registered school. An order form for promotional materials and incentives is included. These items may also be purchased at the Bluebonnet Booth at the TLA conference. It is advantageous to register prior to September, so that promotional materials can be fully utilized. The Aldine district provides certificates of participation which are available from the Director of Library Media Services.

Voting—Voting is conducted in the schools and is directed by the school librarian. Any appropriate date in January is selected as voting day by the participating school. Voting materials, mailed by January 1, are sent to each registered school. Schools duplicate the ballot for use by students eligible to vote. The school wide totals, recorded on an official tally sheet are mailed to the TBA coordinator and must be postmarked on or before January 31. The winner of the Texas Bluebonnet Award is announced in February through a variety of communications, including the TLA–TBA website.

TEXAS LONE STAR READING PROGRAM The Texas Lone Star Reading Program is sponsored by the Young Adult Round Table of the Texas Library Association for students in grades 6–8. An annual master list of twenty books is selected by a Lone Star Reading Committee.

This program is designed to encourage students in grades 6–8 to explore a variety of current books, and to become self-motivated readers of entertaining, quality literature from a variety of genres. The program structure, incentives, and activities will vary from library to library.

AUTHORS/SPEAKERS The Library Media Center often sponsors speakers for the purpose of encouraging reading on the part of district students. When the arrangements involve financial remuneration, the speaker must complete a Contractual Service Agreement. [revised June 1999; www.aldine.k12.tx.us]

Longview (Texas) Independent School District

Handbook of Policies and Procedures for Library Services K–12

The Library Resource Center Program The library media center program develops and implements five services:

1. Instruction of students in the skills necessary to utilize media and library media centers
2. Student and teacher access and services to facilitate learning (both current and life-long)
3. Assistance to teachers and students in materials production
4. Provision of reference and bibliographic services
5. Consultation assistance and in-service education to teachers

LIBRARY INSTRUCTION One of the primary responsibilities of the librarian is instruction in the use of the resources of the library. Students need to learn how to use library media; they need to learn the joy of reading and the quest for knowledge. Skills introduced in the elementary grades are reviewed, expanded, and constantly applied as the students advance in school. They are an integral part of instruction in the content subjects. Students develop independent skills through practice and functional use of library media.

Library staff members have many resources at their disposal to aid in effective library instruction. These include media from the professional library and the video collection. Librarians keep lessons plans reflecting their activities. These lesson plans should be made with the cooperation of the classroom teacher so that library skills may be effectively integrated with the curriculum. [1997–1998 edition; 1301 E. Young Street, Longview, TX 75602]

Chapter Nineteen

Appendixes in Policies

Appendixes serve much the same purpose in collection development policies as in books and other formats, that is, they supply useful supplementary material that has been deemed inappropriate for placement within the main text. There are a number of reasons that may dictate this decision, all of which are concerned with disruption in the narrative flow or exposition of ideas:

- The material is of considerable length, and is hard to understand if presented in truncated form.
- The material, while germane to issues covered in the core policy, may include extraneous details or a somewhat different central thrust.
- The material may be organized in a completely different format, for example, a form, legal document, chart, budget sheet, and so on.

School libraries vary considerably regarding their use of appendixes; some ignore them altogether, whereas others include many entries at the end of the policy. If incorporated into collection development statements, it is imperative that all material be clearly labeled under the heading "appendixes" in the table of contents. Headings in the table of contents should match those in the actual appendixes. Continuous pagination should be employed from the beginning through to the end of the policy, including the appendixes.

SAMPLE POLICIES

Longview (Texas) Independent School District

Handbook of Policies and Procedures for Library Services K–12

Appendix A: Board Policy Regarding Materials Selection & Adoption

Exhibit 1: Citizen's Request for Reconsideration of Instructional Materials
Exhibit 2: Checklist for Reconsideration of Instructional Resources
Exhibit 3: Library Bill of Rights

Appendix B: Board Policy Regarding Copyrighted Material

Fair Use
Broadcast Programs
Rented VCR Tapes
Computer Software
Guidelines for Classroom Copying
Guidelines for Educational Uses of Music

Appendix C: LISD Forms

Exhibit 1: Purchase Requisition
Exhibit 2: Warehouse Requisition
Exhibit 3: Longview ISD Equipment Repair Order
Exhibit 4: Notice of Break-In/Vandalism

Appendix D: Library Forms

L-01 Daily Circulation Tally Sheet
L-02 Monthly Report
L-03 Circulation Summary Report
L-04 School Library Inventory
L-05 Materials Inventory
L-06 Master Heading List
L-07 School Inventory of AV Equipment
L-08 Inventory of Encyclopedias
L-09 Requisition for Library Books
L-10 School Library Expenditures
L-11 Closing Form
L-12 Inventory Corrections

L-13 ITV Video Request/Evaluation
L-14 Video Program Request/Evaluation
L-15 Film Evaluation
L-16 Library Media Specialist Appraisal Form

Appendix E: Appleworks Spread Sheets

Book Inventory
Materials Inventory
Equipment Inventory
Equipment Checking Using Inventory
Software Classification and Processing

Appendix F: Library Curriculum Guide [1997–1998 edition; 1301 E. Young Street, Longview, TX 75602]

Squires Elementary School (Fayette County, Kentucky) Library

Collection Development & Material Selection Policy

Appendix 1: Library Bill of Rights
Appendix 2: Diversity in Collection Development
Appendix 3: Challenged Material

[www.squires.fayette.k12.ky.us/library/collect.htm]

Chapter Twenty

Bibliography

While it seems likely that the majority of collection development policies were created—and revised—with the assistance of other information sources, rarely are these materials cited either directly in document passages or in a separate bibliography. Rather than any aversion to giving credit where credit is due, policy compilers may simply feel these devices represent unnecessary scholarly trappings for what is essentially a practical manual. Nevertheless, where included, bibliographies can serve a number of very useful functions:

- They lend an aura of authority, indicating that the points made within the policy were obtained from reputable sources.
- They draw attention to the professional literature on collection development in general as well as specific issues such as intellectual freedom, weeding guidelines, and the assessment of library holdings. As a result, anyone consulting the policy would have a pathfinder for obtaining more in-depth information on a particular topic of interest.
- They provide a link to standards, forms, policies, and procedures that are germane to a library's collection building program.

SAMPLE POLICIES

Calgary (Alberta, Canada) Board of Education

Guidelines for Evaluation of Learning Resources

Selected References

Ahmad, Nyla (1996). *Cybersurfer: The Owl Internet Guide for Kids*. Toronto: Owl Books.

Bank, Molly (1991). *Picture This: Perception and Composition.* Boston: Little, Brown.

England, Vlaire (1987). *Childview: Evaluating and Reviewing Materials for Children.* Littleton, CO: Libraries Unlimited.

Horning, Kathleen T. (1997). *From Cover to Cover: Evaluating and Reviewing Children's Books.* Toronto: HarperCollins.

Huck, Charlotte (1993). *Children's Literature in the Elementary School.* Toronto: Holt, Rinehart and Winston.

Silvey, Anita (1995). *Children's Books and Their Creators.* Boston: Houghton Mifflin. [published March 1998; http://cbe.ab.cal]

School District of Philadelphia Library Programs and Services

Selection Policy for School Library Materials

Bibliography

Office for Intellectual Freedom, comp. *Intellectual Freedom Manual.* 4th edition. Chicago: American Library Association, 1992.

Reichman, H. *Censorship and Selection: Issues and Answers for Schools.* Chicago: American Library Association, 1993.

Van Orden, Phyllis J. *The Collection Policy Program in Schools.* 2nd edition. Englewood, CO: Libraries Unlimited, 1995. [adopted November 15, 1996 by the Philadelphia Board of Education; revised February 5, 2002; www.libraries.phila.k12.pa.us/misc/selection-policy.html]

Chapter Twenty-One

Acceptable Use Policies

An acceptable use policy (AUP) represents a written agreement, based on guidelines, that is signed by students, educators, and parents, outlining the terms and conditions of online behavior and access privileges.[1] These agreements became widely utilized in the latter half of the 1990s as a means of outlining proper use of site and district-wide computer networks and the Internet for the school community.

Many state departments of education and professional associations openly recommend the development and implementation of acceptable use policies in school environments. These agencies typically provide primers for the creation of AUPs, including checklists or templates for document components. For example, the Virginia Department of Education states that the following sections are typically included in AUPs:

- a description of the instructional philosophies and strategies to be supported by Internet access in schools;
- a statement on the educational uses and advantages of the Internet in your school or division;
- a list of the responsibilities of educators, parents, and students for using the Internet;
- a code of conduct governing behavior on the Internet;
- a description of the consequences of violating the AUP;
- a description of what constitutes acceptable and unacceptable use of the Internet;
- a disclaimer absolving the school division, under specific circumstances, from responsibility;
- a statement reminding users that Internet access and the use of computer networks is a privilege;

- a statement that the AUP is in compliance with state and national telecommunication rules and regulations; and
- a signature form for teachers, parents, and students indicating their intent to abide by the AUP.[2]

STATE REQUIREMENTS FOR PUBLIC SCHOOL INTERNET ACCEPTABLE USE POLICIES AND GUIDELINES

Indiana's education division not only advocates AUPs, but has strongly recommended the format such a document should follow.

A. Each public school corporation in Indiana *must* adopt an Internet Acceptable Use Policy which
  1. describes general instructional philosophies and strategies to be supported by Internet access in the schools
  2. describes the process for governing local Internet system security, user accounts, and user privileges
  3. describes sanctions to be taken when violations of the policy occur
  4. makes specific reference to prohibiting the use of school corporation Internet resources/accounts to
     a. access, upload, download, or distribute pornographic, obscene, or sexually explicit material
     b. transmit obscene, abusive, or sexually explicit language
     c. violate any local, state, or federal statute
     d. vandalize, damage, or disable the property of another person or organization
     e. access another person's materials, information, or files without the implied or direct permission of that person
     f. violate copyright, or otherwise use another person's intellectual property without their prior approval or proper citation
  5. requires that parents be notified that their students will be using school corporation resources/accounts to access the Internet, and provides parents the option to request alternative activities not requiring Internet access
  6. requires the permission of and supervision by the school's professional staff for a student to use a school account or resource to access the Internet
  7. indicates that the educational value of student Internet access is the joint responsibility of students, parents, and employees of the school corporation

8. makes the school corporation's Internet policies and procedures available for review by all parents, guardians, staff, and members of the community
B. Each public school corporation in Indiana *must* provide staff and student Internet users guidelines for
   1. responding to unsolicited online contact; and
   2. safeguarding personal information, such as name, address, telephone number, etc.[3]

Acceptable use policies are generally promulgated as a separate document rather than as a component of school library collection development policies. This makes sense when one considers that AUPs are aimed at all aspects of computer use, whether in the classroom, technology labs, or the library. However, because the information resources comprising today's school media center are heavily reliant upon Internet sites and computer-related software and data files, the collection development policy should—if not including the entire text of the AUP—refer the user to that source.

SAMPLE POLICIES

All of the AUPs below delineate—in varying degrees of depth—the role of technology with the particular institution's educational mission. Both the Corpus Christi Education Service Center and the Los Angeles Unified School District provide sample agreement forms to be signed by various constituent groups. The latter's AUP includes an interesting idea rarely included by other educational institutions, namely, an ethics comprehension exam to be administered to students prior to granting Internet use privileges.

Edmonton (Alberta, Canada) Public Schools

Board Policies and Regulations

Appropriate Use of District Technology

A. Purposeful Use of District Technology
   1. Students will be given access to district technology for educational purposes that include
      • achieving the learner outcomes of the Alberta Program of Studies;
      • participating in learning activities selected by the teacher; and
      • participating in alternate district programs such as virtual schooling and outreach programs.

2. Staff will be given access to district technology for educational purposes that include
   - communication;
   - information acquisition;
   - information management, such as student and financial information;
   - professional development and training; and
   - providing technology support to other users of district technology.
3. Community volunteers and school council representatives may be given access to district technology for educational purposes that include
   - communication;
   - information acquisition; and
   - assisting teachers in using district technology with students.

B. Guiding Principles

District technology must be used in ways that are consistent with the following principles:

1. Appropriate use

   District technology is intended for educational purposes and for business activities in the operation of schools and the district. Personal use of electronic communication must not interfere with, or conflict with, its use for work purposes. District technology cannot be used for purposes that are illegal, unethical, or immoral.

2. Privacy and personal safety

   Activities involving district technology will, as much as possible, protect the privacy of personal information of all users and the personal safety of students. All users will be educated about ways that they can protect their own personal information and personal safety.

3. Security of systems and information

   Individuals using district technology shall not compromise the security and integrity of data and information stored on district or school computer systems.

4. Efficiency

   District technology must function efficiently for all users. Therefore, users shall operate within the limitations, guidelines, and directives provided.

C. Guidelines for Appropriate Use

1. Students and staff shall adhere to appropriate use guidelines established by the district and each school.

2. Schools may request that students and their parents or guardians sign an appropriate use agreement that confirms their understanding of school and district guidelines.

D. Consequences of Inappropriate Use
   1. All users shall be responsible and accountable for their use of district technology.
   2. Students who deliberately use district technology inappropriately will be subject to some or all of the consequences listed in the section, Student Behavior and Conduct.
   3. Staff who deliberately use district technology inappropriately will be subject to disciplinary or legal action, which may include termination of employment.
   3. Other users who deliberately use district technology inappropriately will lose the privilege of using district technology.

[issued May 23, 2000; http://epsb.edmonton.ab.ca/policy/kc.ar.shthl]

Education Service Center, Region 2 (Corpus Christi, Texas)

Network Acceptance Use Guidelines

Network Definition The ESC-2 "Network" consists of computer workstations (MAC and Windows-based), local area network (LAN) resources, the Internet, electronic mail (e-mail), and associated software applications.

Network Goals The goal of the Education Service Center, Region 2 (ESC-2) Network is to increase productivity, disseminate information, ease communication, and promote collaboration. These activities will occur to benefit K–12 educators, the Texas Education Agency (TEA), ESC-2 employees, and other educational entities and supporting organizations.

Network Use All use of the ESC-2 Network shall be consistent with the mission of ESC-2. Successful operation of the Network requires that its users regard the Network and assigned e-mail accounts as professional "property." Each e-mail account is assigned to one authorized individual and is provided for the exclusive use of this individual. It is imperative that users conduct themselves in a responsible, ethical, and polite manner while using e-mail and other aspects of the ESC-2 Network.

Network Acceptable Use Guidelines The intent of the ESC-2 Acceptable Use Guidelines (AUG) is to ensure that all uses of the services provided by the Network are consistent with the goals stated above. These guidelines do not attempt to articulate all required or proscribed behavior by its users. In any specific situation, each individual must rely on her or his own judgment of appropriate conduct.

To assist in such judgment, the following general guidelines are offered:

1. The ESC-2 Network must be used to support education and research.
2. Use of the Network for illegal purposes, or in support of illegal activities, is prohibited.
3. Commercial use of the Network (such as product advertisement or solicitation) is prohibited.
4. Political lobbying via the Network is prohibited.
5. Use of the Network must not disrupt the use of the Network by other users.
6. An e-mail account must be used only by the authorized user.

Violation of these guidelines may result in termination of Network privileges. ESC-2 reserves the right to pursue theft of e-mail services and Network resources. ESC-2 reserves the right to impose fines, as defined by law, for the deliberate misuse of the Network resulting in the violation of personal rights and/or damage to property. Periodically, ESC-2 will make decisions on whether specific uses of the Network are consistent with these guidelines.

I hereby acknowledge that I have received, read, and understand the above Network Acceptable Use Guidelines.

Employee Name (please print)

Social Security Number

Signature

Date

Please return form to the ESC-2 administration. [www.esc2.net/people/esc2aup .htm]

Los Angeles Unified School District

Acceptable Use Policy (AUP) for the Internet

Attachment A

REASONS FOR THIS POLICY The Los Angeles Unified School District is providing computer network and Internet access for its students and employees. This service allows employees and students to share information, learn new concepts, research diverse subjects, and create and maintain school-based websites.

The School District has adopted this Acceptable Use Policy to set guidelines for accessing the computer network or the Internet service provided by the School District. Every year, students and employees who want computer network and Internet access for that upcoming school year need to sign and submit this Policy to the School District. Students who are under 18 also must have their parents or guardians sign this Policy. By signing this agreement, the student, employee, and parent or guardian agree to follow the rules set forth in this Policy and to report any misuse of the computer network or the Internet to a teacher or supervisor. Parties agreeing to this policy also understand the School District may revise the Internet Acceptable Use Policy as it deems necessary. The School District will provide notice of any changes either by posting such a revised version of the Policy on its website or by providing written notice to the students, employees, and parents or guardians.

To obtain free computer network and Internet access, students also must successfully complete the Student Internet Test and follow any school procedures developed at the school site. Each student or employee who qualifies may access the computer network or Internet. This Acceptable Use Policy must accompany any request for a LAUSDnet account (which provides district mail and dial-up access) and is also required for access to any LAUSD network and LAUSD dial-up service. The student or employee is required to change the password the first time he or she uses the Account and routinely thereafter. The Account may only be used during the time the user is a student or employee of the School District. Anyone who receives an Account is responsible for making sure it is used properly.

ACCEPTABLE USES OF THE COMPUTER NETWORK OF THE INTERNET The Account provided by the School District should be used only for educational or professional purposes. Staff may use the Internet for personal use only if such use is incidental and occurs during their duty-free time. If a user is uncertain about whether a particular use of the computer network or the Internet is appropriate, he or she should consult a teacher or supervisor.

UNACCEPTABLE USES OF THE COMPUTER NETWORK OF THE INTERNET The following uses of the Account provided by the School District are unacceptable.

- Uses that violate any state or federal law or federal or municipal ordinance are unacceptable. Unacceptable uses include, but are not limited to the following:
  1. selling or purchasing any illegal substance;
  2. accessing, transmitting, or downloading child pornography, obscene depictions, harmful materials, or materials that encourage others to violate the law; or
  3. transmitting or downloading confidential information or copyrighted materials.

- Uses that involve the accessing, transmitting or downloading of inappropriate matters on the Internet, as determined by the school board, local educational agency or other related authority
- Uses that involve obtaining and or using anonymous email sites
- Uses that cause harm to others or damage to their property are unacceptable. Unacceptable uses include, but are not limited to the following:

    1. deleting, copying, modifying, or forging other users' e-mails, files, or data;
    2. accessing another user's e-mail without their permission, and as a result of that access, reading or forwarding the other user's e-mails or files without that user's permission;
    3. damaging computer equipment, files, data, or the network;
    4. using profane, abusive, or impolite language;
    5. disguising one's identity, impersonating other users, or sending anonymous e-mail messages;
    6. threatening, harassing, or making defamatory or false statements about others;
    7. accessing, transmitting, or downloading offensive, harassing or disparaging materials;
    8. accessing, transmitting, or downloading computer viruses or other harmful files or programs, or in any way degrading or disrupting any computer system performance;
    9. accessing, transmitting or downloading large files, including "chain letters" or any type of "pyramid schemes"; or
    10. using any district computer to pursue "hacking," internal or external to the district, or attempting to access information that is protected by privacy laws.

- Uses that jeopardize access or lead to unauthorized access into Accounts or other computer networks, including

    1. using other users' account passwords or identifiers;
    2. disclosing one's account password to other users or allowing other users to use one's accounts;
    3. getting unauthorized access into other users' accounts or other computer networks; or
    4. interfering with other users' ability to access their accounts.

- Commercial uses, including

    1. selling or buying anything over the Internet for personal financial gain;
    2. using the Internet for advertising, promotion, or financial gain; or

3. conducting for-profit business activities and engaging in non-government related fundraising or public relations activities such as solicitation for religious purposes, lobbying for political purposes, or soliciting votes.

INTERNET SAFETY   In compliance with the Children's Internet Protection Act (CIPA), the School District will implement filtering and/or blocking software to restrict access to Internet sites containing child pornography, obscene depictions, or other materials harmful to minors under 18 years of age. The software will work by scanning for objectionable words or concepts, as determined by the School District. [Note: CIPA does not enumerate any actual words or concepts that should be filtered or blocked. Thus, CIPA necessarily requires that the School District determine which words or concepts are objectionable.] However, no software is foolproof, and there is still a risk an Internet user may be exposed to a site containing such materials. An account user who incidentally connects to such a site must immediately disconnect from the site and notify a teacher or supervisor. If an account user sees another user is accessing inappropriate sites, he or she should notify a teacher or supervisor immediately.

In compliance with CIPA, the School District and its representatives will implement a mechanism to monitor all minors' online activities, including website browsing, e-mail use, chat room participation, and other forms of electronic communications. Such a mechanism may lead to the discovery that a user has violated or may be violating this policy, the appropriate disciplinary code, or the law. Monitoring is aimed to protect minors from accessing inappropriate matter, as well as to help enforce this policy on the Internet, as determined by the school board, local educational agency or other related authority. The School District reserves the right to monitor other users' (e.g., employees, students seventeen years or older) online activities, and to access, review, copy, store, or delete any electronic communications or files and disclose them to others as it deems necessary.

If a student under the age of 18 accesses his/her LAUSDnet Account or the Internet outside of school, a parent or legal guardian must supervise the student's use of the Internet account at all times and is completely responsible for monitoring the use. Filtering and/or blocking software may or may not be employed to screen home access to the Internet. Parents and legal guardians should inquire at the school or district if they desire more detailed information about the software.

Student information shall not be posted unless it is necessary to receive information for instructional purposes, and only if the student's teacher and parent or guardian has granted permission.

Account users shall not reveal on the Internet personal information about themselves or about other persons. For example, account users should not reveal their full names, home addresses, telephone numbers, school addresses, or parents' names on the Internet.

Account users shall not meet in person anyone they have met on the Internet in a secluded place or private setting. Account users who are under the age of 18 shall not meet in person anyone they have met on the Internet without their parents' permission.

Account users will abide by all school district security policies.

PRIVACY POLICY   The System Administrator has the authority to monitor all accounts, including e-mail and other materials transmitted or received via the accounts. All such materials are the property of the School District. Account users do not have any right to or expectation of privacy regarding such materials.

STORAGE CAPACITY   To ensure that account users remain within the allocated disk space, users with e-mail accounts should check their e-mail frequently and delete unwanted messages and other files or data that take up excessive storage space. The System Administrator will also routinely delete messages from account users' inbound and outbound log files, messages saved to the archive folders on the system, and messages posted to the School District's web site.

PENALTIES FOR IMPROPER USE   The use of the account is a privilege, not a right, and inappropriate use will result in the restriction or cancellation of the account. Inappropriate use may lead to disciplinary and/or legal action, including but not limited to suspension or expulsion or dismissal from employment from the School District, or criminal prosecution by government authorities. The School District will attempt to tailor any disciplinary action to meet the specific concerns related to each violation.

DISCLAIMER   The School District makes no guarantees about the quality of the services provided and is not responsible for any claims, losses, damages, costs, or other obligations arising from the unauthorized use of the accounts. The School District also denies any responsibility for the accuracy or quality of the information obtained through the account.

Any statement, accessible on the computer network or the Internet, is understood to be the author's individual point of view and not that of the School District, its affiliates, or employees.

Account users are responsible for any losses sustained by the School District or its affiliates, resulting from the account users' intentional misuse of the accounts.

For further information, please call the LAUSDnet Unit at (213) 241-1212.

Attachment B: Employment Agreement   All active employees must read and sign below.

I have read, understand, and agree to abide by the provisions of the attached Acceptable Use Policy of the Los Angeles Unified School District.

I understand and agree in the event a third party makes a claim against the School District as a result of my use of the computer network or the Internet provided by the School District, the School District reserves its right to respond to such a claim as it sees fit and to hold all offending parties, including myself, responsible.

I release the School District, its affiliates, and its employees from any claims or damages of any nature arising from my access or use of the computer network or the Internet provided by the School District. I am responsible for toll charges (if any) as a result of using LAUSDnet services. I also agree not to hold the School District responsible for materials improperly acquired on the system or for violations of copyright restrictions, users' mistakes or negligence, or any costs incurred by users.

This agreement shall be governed by and construed under the laws of the United States and the State of California.

_____	_____
Employee Name	Employee No.
_____	_____
Employee Signature	Date

This form is to be kept at the school or office and kept on file by the school site administrator. It is required for all employees that will be using a computer network and/or Internet access. It is to be renewed each year prior to any computer network or Internet usage.

Attachment C: Student Agreement All active students, regardless of age, must read and sign below.

I have read, understand, and agree to abide by the provisions of the attached Acceptable Use Policy of the Los Angeles Unified School District.

I understand and agree in the event that a third party makes a claim against the School District as a result of my use of the computer network or the Internet provided by the School District, the School District reserves its right to respond to such a claim as it sees fit and to hold all offending parties, including myself, responsible.

I release the School District, its affiliates, and its employees from any claims or damages of any nature arising from my access or use of the computer network or the Internet provided by the School District. I am responsible for toll charges (if any) as a result of using LAUSDnet services. I also agree not to hold the School District responsible for materials improperly acquired on the system or for violations of copyright restrictions, users' mistakes or negligence, or any costs incurred by users.

This agreement shall be governed by and construed under the laws of the United States and the State of California.

School	Location Code
Student Name	10-Digit Student ID Number
Student Signature	Date

The student completed the Student Internet Test on the following date: _____

Name of Teacher-Sponsor (for Student Users)

This form is to be kept at the school site and kept on file by the classroom teacher or school site administrator. It is required for all students that will be using a computer network and/or Internet access. It is to be renewed each year prior to any computer network or Internet usage.

Attachment D: Parent Or Guardian Agreement   All parents or legal guardians of students under 18 must read and sign below.

As the parent or legal guardian of the above student, I have read, understand, and agree my child or dependent must comply with the provisions of the attached Acceptable Use Policy of the Los Angeles Unified School District. I give full permission to the School District to give my child or dependent access to a LAUSDnet Account and to the LAUSDnet system.

I accept full responsibility for the supervision of my child or dependent's use of his/her LAUSDnet Account and the Internet at home or while not in a school setting. I understand and agree in the event a third party makes a claim against the School District as a result of my child or dependent's use of the computer network or the Internet provided by the School District, the School District reserves its right to respond to such a claim as it sees fit and to hold all offending parties, including my child or dependent, responsible.

I release the School District, its affiliates, and its employees from any claims or damages of any nature arising from my child or dependent's access or use of the computer network of the Internet provided by the School district. I am responsible for toll charges (if any) as a result of using LAUSDnet services. I also agree not to hold the School District responsible for materials improperly acquired on the system, or for violations of copyright restrictions, users' mistakes or negligence, or any costs incurred by users.

This agreement shall be governed by and construed under the laws of the United States and the State of California.

_____

School

_____

Name of Student

_____

Parent/Legal Guardian Name

_____   _____

Parent/Legal Guardian Signature   Date

This form is to be kept at the school site and kept on file by the classroom teacher or school site administrator. It is required for all students that will be using a computer network and/or Internet access. It is to be renewed each year prior to any computer network or Internet usage.

Attachment E: Site Agreement   All school site administrators providing access to students and employees must sign below.

As the site administrator, I have read, understand, and agree. The employees I supervise and the students at my location have submitted the signed appropriate agreement (*Student Agreement, Parent Agreement,* or *Employee Agreement*) and they are on file at my site. I understand these procedures must be updated annually and must be kept on file at my location.

I understand and agree in the event that a third party makes a claim against the School District as a result of my use of the computer network or the Internet provided by the School District, the School District reserves its right to respond to such a claim as it sees fit and to hold all offending parties, including myself, responsible.

The agreement shall be governed by and construed under the laws of the United States and the State of California.

_____

Date

_____   _____

School Site   Location Code

_____   _____

Principal/Site Administrator   Principal's Signature

_____   _____

School Telephone Number   School Fax Number

This form is to be submitted to the LAUSDnet Unit and a copy kept on file by the school site administrator. It is required for all district locations that use computer network and/or Internet access. It is to be renewed each year prior to any computer network or Internet usage.

Attachment F: Student Internet Test   Note: If a student is unable to read the Internet Test, a teacher may assist by reading the questions and marking the answers. This "test" is a tool to teach Internet etiquette, NOT a test to exclude anyone. If a student does not pass the test, the issues should be discussed and the test given again.

MULTIPLE CHOICE (CIRCLE THE CORRECT ANSWER):

1. A student or teacher may use his or her LAUSDnet account to
   a) sell something
   b) hack other systems on the Internet
   c) do research for a class project
   d) illegally download software
   e) harm another individual
2. Sharing passwords is
   a) strictly prohibited
   b) acceptable among your closest friends
   c) acceptable among fellow students working on a class project
   d) always a good idea
   e) allowed if you change your password frequently
3. Deleting unwanted files and e-mails from your LAUSDnet account is
   a) recommended but not necessary
   b) not an issue because there is unlimited disk space
   c) required because disk space is limited
   d) only done when my teacher asks me to
   e) never done
4. If you think that someone is using your password, you should
   a) change your password
   b) notify your teacher
   c) notify abuse @lausd.k12.ca.us
   d) not worry about it
   e) a, b, and c
5. When using e-mail, you
   a) may send offensive letters
   b) may send e-mail to people you do not know
   c) may never know who is reading your mail
   d) must follow the Acceptable Use Policy
   e) c and d
6. If you need help
   a) ask your technology teacher
   b) look for help on the Internet
   c) ask your teacher

  d) all of the above
  e) none of the above
7. If I violate the Acceptable Use Policy, I could
  a) be required to attend a disciplinary meeting at my school with my parents
  b) lose my LAUSDnet account
  c) be suspended from school
  d) face possible arrest and prosecution
  e) all of the above

[BULLETIN NO. K-19, revised March 15, 2002; www.lausd.k12.ca.us/lausd/lausdnet/aup.html]

Red Deer (Alberta, Canada) Public School District

District Network and Internet Agreement for Independent Student Use

The Red Deer Public School District has installed a Wide Area Network connecting all of its schools together. Included in the services available on the district network is access to the Internet for students and staff. The district strongly believes in the educational value of such electronic services and their potential in promoting educational excellence by facilitating sharing of resources, access to information, innovation, global communication and collaboration. By helping education extend beyond the classroom, this network will enhance the ability of teachers and students to meet the challenges of the future.

  With access to computers and people from all over the world, also comes the availability of material that may not be considered to be of educational value in the context of the school setting. Red Deer Public School District #104 has taken precautions to restrict access to controversial materials from the Internet. However, on a global network, it is impossible to control all materials and an industrious user may discover controversial information. We firmly believe that the valuable information and interaction available on this worldwide network far outweighs the possibility that users may procure material that is not consistent with the educational goals of the Red Deer Public School District #104.

District Guidelines for Student Use of the District Network and the Internet

Students are expected to use the district network and the Internet as an educational resource. The following procedures and guidelines have been established to ensure sound and productive educational experiences.

- Students receive instruction in the proper access to and use of district network and Internet resources as well as instruction in information research skills appropriate for their age group.
- At school, all Internet use focuses on the attainment of instructional goals as established by the classroom teacher.
- All computers used by students are equipped with filtering software to block, as much as possible, access to Internet material inappropriate in a school setting.
- Student access to the Internet is guided and supervised by the classroom teacher.
- Access to Internet USENET newsgroups as well as Internet Relay Chat is limited to teacher computers and therefore is available to students only under supervised conditions.
- Access to browser-based e-mail and CHAT lists is enabled for high school students only.
- At the elementary and middle school level, student e-mail accounts are only issued for teacher-directed group projects, and only for the duration of such projects.
- At this time, student e-mail accounts are only issued for teacher-directed group projects at the high school level, and only for the duration of such projects.
- Students are responsible for their use of the district network and their explorations of the Internet and are subject to disciplinary actions in the event of inappropriate and unacceptable use of its resources.
- Parents must give permission for their child to use the Internet independently for educational purposes, by signing the Parent Permission Form. The district supports and respects the parent's right to decide whether or not to apply for independent access.

Student Responsibilities: Use of the District Network and the Internet

Students are responsible for good behavior on district computer networks just as they are in their school. Internet access is a privilege—not a right! It is provided to conduct research and to communicate with others. Inappropriate use will result in cancellation of these privileges and may result in additional disciplinary or legal actions.

The following activities are prohibited on the Red Deer Public School District network:

- Engaging in illegal, unethical, or malicious acts
- Accessing resources without authorization inside or outside of the district network

- Sending files or messages to disrupt other computer systems or networks
- Composing, sending, or storing messages which include profanity, sexual, racial, religious, or ethnic slurs or other abuse, threatening or otherwise offensive language or pictures
- Using a home e-mail account to access Internet materials with school computers
- Possessing, using, or transmitting unauthorized material (i.e., copyright protected)
- Downloading large files during school hours (bandwidth limitations)
- Revealing personal information of themselves or their friends over the Internet
- Trespassing in another person's folders, work, or files
- Intentionally wasting printing resources
- Using the district/school network for non-educational purposes

It is critical to the security of the Red Deer Public School District Network that all users do their part to safeguard the security precautions in place. If any student should discover a security problem on the network, they must notify a school authority at once. Students are prohibited from the following:

- Demonstrating a security problem to other users
- Using another's e-mail account
- Sharing e-mail accounts and passwords

Parent Permission Form District Network and Internet Use Agreement

Sponsoring Teacher   I have read the *District Network and Internet Use Agreement* and agree to promote this agreement with the student. Since the student may use the network for individual work or in the context of another class, I cannot be held responsible for the student's use of the network. As the sponsoring teacher, I do agree to instruct the student on acceptable use of the district network and the Internet.

Teacher's Name: _____

Teacher's Signature: _____   Date: _____

Student   I have received instruction in the acceptable use of the district network and the Internet and I understand my responsibilities pertaining to their appropriate use. I agree to follow the guidelines as outlined in this *District Network and Internet Use Agreement*. Further, I understand that any violation of the above conditions, rules, and this agreement may constitute a suspension of access privileges to the Internet and/or any other consequences as deemed necessary by school authorities.

Student's Name: _____

Student's Signature: _____   Date: _____

Parent or Guardian   (If you are under the age of 18, a parent or guardian must also read and sign this agreement.) As the parent or guardian of this student, I have read the *District Network and Internet Use Agreement*. I understand that this access is designed for educational purposes only. Red Deer Public School District #104 has taken precautions to eliminate controversial material. However, I also recognize it is impossible for the school to restrict access to all offensive materials and I will not hold them responsible for materials acquired on the network. I hereby give permission for my child to independently access the Internet, and certify that the information contained on this form is correct.

Parent or Guardian's Name: _____

Parent or Guardian's Signature: _____   Date: _____

[www.rdpsd.ab.ca/district/districtpages/districtaup.html; www.rdpsd.ab.ca/POLICYSEARCH.htm (then click on "library" and "Policy Manual")]

Saskatoon (Saskatchewan, Canada) Public School Division

Internet Acceptable Use Procedures for Students

1. Access to the Internet is an individual privilege, not a right. Any student who violates these guidelines or any other code of conduct outlined by an individual school will have his or her access removed for such period as is deemed appropriate by a teacher, the teacher librarian, or school administrator.
2. Generally, a student's conduct on the Internet is governed by the same expectation which guide his or her behavior at school.
3. Access to the Internet will only be provided while a student is under the supervision of a teacher or responsible adult who is present in the room where the student is accessing the Internet.
4. Students may not be given access to any passwords necessary to access the Internet.
5. All incidents of accessing inappropriate material will be handled according to the Saskatoon Board of Education Internet Acceptable Use Procedures and individual school guidelines.

6. Students will not use the Internet for purposes other than as requested by a teacher. Frivolous or commercial usage of the Internet is not permitted.
7. Students will not create, distribute, download or save any text, sounds, graphics, or other material which are obscene, harassing, racist, malicious, fraudulent, libelous or which may affect the integrity of a computer or computer network.
8. Students may not attempt to read, copy, or change files or passwords belonging to other people, either locally or on the Internet.
9. All students will participate in an orientation session concerning the acceptable use of the Internet before they may access the Internet.
10. Parents or guardians who do not want their son/daughter to use the Internet at school may sign the Internet Use Denial Form and return it to school.

[copyright 2000; www.sbe.saskatoon.sk.ca/REPORTS/INTERNETAUP .HTML]

NOTES

1. Virginia Department of Education, Division of Technology, "Acceptable Use Policies—A Handbook," www.pen.k12.va.us/go/VDOE/Technology/AUP/home .shtml.
2. Virginia Department of Education, "Acceptable Use Policies."
3. Southern Indiana Education Center, "State Requirements for Public School Internet Acceptable Use Policies and Guidelines," www.siec.k12.in.us/aup/require .html.

Chapter Twenty-Two

Virtual Collection Development

Asking if a virtual database exists if it cannot be located in the library may be somewhat similar to asking if a library book exists when it is hopelessly out of place. Library patrons may not be able to find either if they do not know exactly where to look, but both do exist. A physical book, circulation desk, or magazine issue all have a physical presence in the library that a student, for instance, can see or feel. Even a misplaced library book has a presence. But a virtual resource—like an e-mail or a blog—does not have a physical presence on a library shelf or file cabinet. Unless you count an icon representing the virtual database, or the text of a page from a document in the database that appears on a computer monitor temporarily until another image takes its place, neither the user nor the school librarian can actually handle the content within a virtual database. It is even different than a licensed word-processing or presentation software package that comes on a CD-ROM and must be placed in the disk drive and uploaded to the hard disk on the workstation in order to run. The software can be later removed as well.

Virtual resources differ markedly from physical library resources in how users locate them. A student might intentionally or unintentionally find a magazine or book on library shelves—but cannot make use of Internet resources unless he or she first accesses the World Wide Web from a computer workstation or laptop that provides Internet access. Unless someone instructs a student about how to access a virtual resource, or unless an icon representing it is "visible" on the computer screen, the virtual resource is inaccessible, much like the library book on the wrong shelf. Neither may be used unless the user stumbles upon it. Because more and more students "live" on the Web, a student is perhaps more likely to stumble upon virtual databases and other information or websites than a misplaced library book (or even one in its rightful place on the shelves). So school librarians must be willing to provide Web-accessible library databases if they want to be relevant to students today.

School librarians have always played a vital role in providing information resources for students, teachers, administrators, and other users. Traditionally, this role has been to make physical items such as books, journals, audio, video, and other resources available in an organized and centralized manner so that users can locate them when they visit the library.

Virtual resources have added another dimension to the role of school librarians. Virtual resources have presented school librarians with new challenges and the need for new partnerships. School librarians have become highly dependent upon the technical expertise of other school staff who can provide secure computer access to students, teachers, and others trying to access licensed databases from Internet-accessible computers. Instructional, marketing, preservation, and other challenges—which fall outside the scope of this book—also add to the importance of partnerships for school librarians. Certainly, the concept or very definition of the school library has changed, or needs to change, to reflect an ever-changing and dynamic information environment.

The scenario described above is the reason the authors contend that a separate collection development policy for virtual resources is needed. The components of a policy statement for virtual resources are fundamentally different from those of traditional physical resources, including CD-ROMs and DVDs. The authors also favor a separate statement on virtual resources because doing so makes for a clearer and easier to understand comprehensive collection development policy. Having a policy that covers both physical and virtual resources also should help school administrators, teachers, parents, and others who might read it in its entirety to understand the inherent differences between them. The kinds of differences discussed in this chapter may be difficult for nonlibrarians to understand, but a carefully presented policy statement for virtual resources will help readers understand the information environment. A separate statement on virtual resources should make it clear to all concerned, particularly school administrators and trustees, that the school library has become reliant on those who maintain campus computer and telecommunications systems. Such systems must include the development of a safe and secure computer network that allows users to be authenticated and validated in order to comply with the license agreements of database vendors.

Now that a large percentage of the population in the United States have Internet-accessible computers and know how to access information through search engines such as Google, some say that the physical library is, or is rapidly becoming, a relic of an earlier decade. While school librarians know this is a patently false perception, the concern must nonetheless be addressed. Maintaining a physical library with books, journals, films, and Internet-accessible workstations for students is important, but a well-developed virtual collection development policy is another way to prevent this perception from becoming a reality. The importance of a comprehensive policy, therefore, should not be underestimated.

Students, parents, teachers, and school administrators who read the virtual resources policy will realize that school librarians are reinventing themselves as essential information managers in a world that is producing billions of gigabytes of new content every year. School librarians must play a role in connecting students with both physical and virtual resources because they now surpass print-only material as the source of most of the content. But the school library should always be the physical and metaphysical center of knowledge and information on campus. The school librarian's role, perhaps more importantly, is to continuously adapt to a constantly changing technological and information environment that library users often find overwhelming to navigate.

In volume 1 of *Library Collection Development Policies: Academic, Public, and Special Libraries* (Scarecrow Press, 2005), we titled the next chapter "Policy Component for *Electronic* Resources." In this volume, we title it "Policy Components for *Virtual Resources*" in an effort to be more precise. More importantly, we wish to make a clear distinction between virtual and electronic resources. This begs the question: What are the attributes that distinguish "virtual" from "electronic" and "nonelectronic" resources? A thorough discussion in the policy statement is recommended in order to set the stage for introducing virtual resources and virtual collection development.

It is prudent to distinguish between "electronic" and "nonelectronic" resources before trying to define what we mean by "virtual" resources. Electronic media most often involve the use of electrons as the semiconducting material. This could include music that is produced by electronic means such as a tape recorder. Individuals, educators, commercial entities—anyone with appropriate computer hardware and software can produce or manipulate photographic images, music, and video recordings, then "burn" them to CD-ROMs or DVDs. Costs of such hardware and software has become so reasonable that many homes and offices are equipped to produce such electronic resources. Consumers have Adobe Photoshop and Roxio Easy Media Creator, or many other software programs to manipulate images, video, and audio. Commercial entities differ mostly in the quality of the hardware, software, and professional staff used to produce very high quality products in large quantities.

NONELECTRONIC (PHYSICAL) SCHOOL LIBRARY RESOURCES

Nonelectronic resources are certainly very familiar to most consumers because they include the physical objects that libraries house on shelves: printed books, documents, pamphlets, and serial publications (e.g., magazines, journals, newspapers, and newsletters). Serials have been "imaged" and made available in microfilm and microfiche formats to save space. They generally contain photographic images of journal articles, documents, newspapers, or other text. Few school libraries today continue to acquire micromedia for reasons that we shall explain shortly when discussing archival aspects of virtual full-text journal databases.

Other physical, nonelectronic formats have long been housed on school library shelves or in special storage devices for decades. School librarians might now regard most audio and visual materials as "traditional" school library materials because school libraries have housed filmstrips, slides, overhead transparencies, phonograph records, cassette tapes, reel-to-reel tapes, 16mm film, 8mm film loops, games, puzzles, kits or mixed-media, and puppets for decades. School librarians normally refer to such items as "audiovisuals" or "instructional materials." While we cannot enjoin a debate as to whether a particular format should be regarded as traditional or nontraditional in the space allotted here, there is no denying that such materials are "physical" resources.

ELECTRONIC RESOURCES

Advances in computing and telecommunication technologies, particularly since the mid-1980s, gave rise to many innovative electronic products acquired by all types of libraries. Once the cost of personal computer workstations became affordable enough for school libraries to acquire them for student use, it was not long before a host of products developed. Among the first products were portable storage devices such as the floppy disk and CD-ROM, which were capable of storing library catalogs, reference sources, and journal indexes, to name a few. The first electronic format that school librarians might recall using or seeing is the floppy disk, a 5.25" soft product that fit in a floppy drive of the workstation. These were replaced by a harder 3.5" disk that the user could also put in a drive of the workstation. Most school-age children today cannot recall seeing a 5.25" floppy disk and computer drive. If a school library still has a collection of such disks, chances are good that there are no longer workstations with the drives that read them. The same fate was due for the 3.5" disk and disk drive. They are still in use, but no longer come standard with new computer purchases. What led to the death of the 5.25" floppy disk and the 3.5" storage devices was the development of a new type of storage device called the CD-ROM. The CD-ROM is an optical, stamped disk capable of storing 650 megabytes, equivalent to seven hundred floppy discs or about three hundred thousand pages of text. With later advances in scanning technology during the 1990s, any print source can be digitized easily, then "output" to a CD-ROM, DVD, computer hard disk, or server. From the late 1990s, the most popular output for vendors has been to a server that libraries, businesses, institutions, and other customers can access through the Internet.

Once whole dictionaries, encyclopedias, almanacs, and journal indexes could be stored on a single CD-ROM, school librarians began to realize that the stage was set for the liberation from print sources. When CD-ROM products became inexpensive enough for the mass market, librarians also envisioned the "liberation" of the researcher from the physical library. Many librarians feared that CD-ROMs were the beginning of the demise of library collections, if not libraries and librarians themselves. Today, most workstations come with CD-ROM and DVD drives, and many even come with "burners." A burner not only allows the user to read the data saved to the disk, but also save (burn) data, audio, and visual material to a CD-ROM or DVD for playback. In this way, CD-ROMs and DVDs can store all or most of the computer files on the hard drive of a personal workstation, a laptop, or a server as a backup. Some school librarians might remember when library holding records were stored on CD-ROM beginning in the 1980s. This practice largely ended by the early 1990s. Suffice it to say that before 1995, database searching in schools all across the United States was largely limited to workstations housed in a physical library to access a physical, electronic resource.

All of the formats described above have some important common attributes as follows:

- each format represents physical items;
- each item in any of the formats was ordered by the library or gifted to it;
- each item was most likely cataloged and processed for the library's collection;
- each item had to be shelved or stored in the school's library collection; and
- the items could be borrowed from the library by the user or used within the library for reference or viewing and listening.

The selection and evaluation component of the policy for electronic, physical resources should follow the outline for the school's policy dealing with physical materials such as books, audio, visual, and other physical materials. These may include all of the components covered in Chapter 1.

VIRTUAL (NONPHYSICAL) RESOURCES

CD-ROMs were no match for computer servers that vendors could use to store, maintain, and distribute large databases and libraries or their parent institutions could use to gain access to the Internet. Servers ushered in the era of the virtual database to provide access to personal computers. Most school libraries by 2004 also acquired or licensed virtual resources such as full-text article databases, electronic journal subscriptions, and electronic books. What sets these resources apart from all the others we have discussed?

The distinguishing traits of virtual databases are that they are *not physical items*. All virtual resources are electronic and nonphysical insofar as the librarian is concerned. But not all electronic resources are virtual resources because some are physical, for example, CD-ROMs and DVDs. Electronic resources are virtual resources when they cannot be held by a library user or shelved by a librarian. Almost by definition, virtual resources are licensed by a publisher or aggregator and are regarded as a subset of electronic resources because their content is in the form of bits and bytes that are transmitted electronically. Thus, virtual resources cannot be loaned or borrowed because the library does not receive a physical surrogate as a result of ordering them. In fact, most virtual resources must be ordered as a licensed database. The legal, accountable representative of the library, consortium, or state agency that negotiates the license must sign such license agreements.

A number of technological and telecommunication advances since the mid-1990s have provided K–12 students and teachers with access to unprecedented amounts of information by nonphysical means. The rapid and widespread introduction in the 1990s of networked computers that K–12 students could use to access the Internet profoundly changed the nature of information retrieval and searching in school libraries. Simultaneous advances in server technology and affordable pricing for them and for access to the Internet allowed schools, school districts, and local governments to establish telecommunication networks. Funding from grants, private donations, special state or local taxes on phone services, or school operating funds were used to link school libraries, classrooms, and offices to the Internet. As a result, there were efforts all across the United States to develop local and wide area networks (LANs and WANs) whereby e-mail, phone services, and access to common databases were practical.

But it was when any student—anywhere—could access information in databases stored on company or institutional servers through the Internet that profound changes occurred in how the literature could be stored, searched, retrieved, and disseminated directly to the user. The Internet's capabilities are what essentially led to the rapid demise of the CD-ROM and all other physical, electronic media for the distribution of reference sources, full-text databases, and other information by publishers and vendors. While reference sources are still being produced on CD-ROMs and sold to school libraries as of 2007, it is only a matter of time before this format is no longer produced.

One reason for this is that CD-ROMs are physical, nondynamic computer storage devices that require mechanical computer devices to make the data accessible to the user. For all practical purposes, no physical resources are necessary to access a database except for an Internet-accessible computer workstation or laptop.

All of these telecommunication and technological advances made it possible for vendors to offer virtual databases to the schools at attractive prices, particularly when consortium and statewide agreements could be negotiated. Once Internet-accessible workstations were installed in school libraries, classrooms, and offices throughout the campus, the stage was set for virtual collection development.

Publishers, as well as vendors like EBSCO and ProQuest, were very quick to capitalize on advances in scanning or digitization technologies to create databases suitable for the primary, secondary, and postsecondary markets. At first, products were limited to indexing and abstracting tools, so the school market was very limited. When more and more full-text databases were introduced as a result of successful negotiations between the vendors and publishers, it took only a few years for full-text databases of all types to become the norm in schools, colleges, and universities. This was particularly the case where state libraries, statewide consortia, large school districts, or other entities could negotiate multiagency agreements. Efforts by school, public, and academic librarians across states were also crucial to developing statewide license agreements with vendors such as the Gale Group, EBSCO, ProQuest, and NewsBank. Today, school libraries, like their public and academic counterparts, offer their students and teachers a diverse array of Internet-accessible resources.

Google and other companies, libraries, archives, and other entities have implemented wholesale scanning projects to digitize works in the public domain, or materials that they hold the rights to. Google, for example, has recently negotiated profit-sharing deals with publishers to make portions of saleable printed books available to the public. Companies such as EBL, Inc., provide chapters of books to libraries that want to put them on reserve for students to view.

Virtual resources, however, cannot be housed on shelves or in a file cabinet because they are not physical resources. Sure, the data exists somewhere and in some physical form such as computer memory, but the computer server and memory that holds the electronic data or digitized text is accessed remotely by means of the Internet. As a result, school libraries normally license virtual electronic resources such as full-text journal article databases either directly from publishers or through vendors such as EBSCO, ProQuest, and Ovid. Students access the database and its content by means of Web-accessible workstations or laptop computers. Thus, all Web-accessible databases are *virtual* resources because they are not physical resources housed within the library.

When licensed or made accessible through a school library's website, they nonetheless should be regarded as library resources. So, can virtual resources be cataloged and counted as library resources? Most certainly. All accrediting agencies expect libraries to count virtual resources as "owned" by the library. Moreover, every student's search of a database licensed by the school library can and should count as a use of the library. It should be quickly added, however, that it is advisable to track database searches or "hits" as a separate statistic—one quite distinct from a book circulation, interlibrary loan, or other physical material count. It is more than an interesting exercise to graph the total number of hits from year to year and see how the trend line differs from other variables such as circulation, in-library use, interlibrary loans, and photocopies.

This strategy or viewpoint is also consistent with changes that have become very apparent at this writing. One trend deals with how content is being sold by publishers and producers. Music tracks, films, chapters of books, poems, and other traditional print sources are increasingly available through commercial websites on a transaction basis. Games are now very frequently played by individuals of all ages through the Internet in an interactive mode with one or more individuals at a time, depending upon the game. "Gamers" can live in any country; they just have to be signed in to the Internet. It is not clear how this trend will impact the school library.

Another trend is that books, music albums, and other media are being unbundled. Amazon.com, for instance, now sells pages of books for a few cents a page. Ebook Library (EBL) and other service providers sell chapters of books to libraries or teachers; these may be put on electronic reserve for students. These and other providers are eager to meet the growing demand for direct, user-centric selection of the specific content users want, when they want it. So far, Amazon.com has made its service available only to the user, whereas EBL will sell a portion of a text to a library if is placed on electronic reserve. Whether and how libraries figure into the marketing schemes of vendors remains to be seen as this book goes to the editor.

Within a short time, we anticipate that vendors will be offering direct user (student) selection through their company's websites. Students will thus be able to bypass the school library altogether if access through the commercial site is convenient, fast, secure, affordable, and timely. Until the school librarian reviews a product, gets approval to spend the money, makes sure the network administrator does not have a problem with configuring the product to work, and so forth, often there is a time delay of months before students can get access. The movement to allow selection decisions to be made by the user is therefore a very logical next step, because any user normally wants nothing less than a very specific song, film, film clip, image, poem, passage, chapter, or game as quickly and conveniently as possible. Students and other users may want to bypass the websites of libraries and schools, which are likely to have authentication, verification, survey, and other features to ensure security, the capture of use statistics, archiving, and so forth.

Another example of a potentially revolutionary development in the information environment concerns a project by Google and its possible impact on copyright law. As this chapter was being written, Google was implementing Google Print, a plan to digitize and make available to its customers the content of both public domain and authorized copyrighted books. Google has begun to scan the books in several major research libraries, including Harvard, Stanford, and the New York Public Library. Although Google plans to include search results listing copyrighted books, librarians and other educators feel the company is taking a huge risk by including copyrighted books even though only a limited portion of the text may be viewed by users. Google markets the project to publishers by saying that Google Print should greatly enhance the sale of books. The sudden exposure of the public to the knowledge about relevant book titles, Google reasons, will push book sales to new heights. The authors believe this claim might very well be true, but also must express concern that the legal copyright questions be resolved. If what Google Print does is fair use, we do believe that the public will be better served. Nonetheless, it is not prudent to second-guess how the courts will decide these complex legal issues.

Another copyright question that Google tests is its assertion that publishers can opt out, whereas copyright law seems clear that the copyright owner must first give permission for the digitization. Finally, Google itself will not sell books to the consumer, so it will not profit directly.

Google's bold initiative in 2005 produced a lawsuit by the Author's Guild and will undoubtedly lead to additional court cases, the outcomes of which might create a new precedent. The significant legal issue is whether a company like Google can scan a copyrighted work without first getting the permission of the publisher, that is, prior to making it available through Google Print. Publishers also contend that making even a page from an entire book available through Google Print is illegal if permission was not first given by the copyright owner. The interesting facet of such a suit occurs if Google Print does significantly enhance the revenue of publishers and copyright owners. While many publishers have signed agreements with Google permitting the scanning, many publishers have not signed and want to protect their intellectual property rights. Librarians are urged to watch developments with Google Print very closely because the outcome of all the legal suits that are bound to be filed will determine what content library users will be able to access. If Google Print is successful, copyright law would be redefined and many other companies would jump on the bandwagon. Amazon.com, for instance, recently launched a similar program to Google Print called Amazon Pages. There is a lot of income at risk for all concerned as well. Until these legal questions are firmly decided, school librarians may not want to include links to Google Print on their websites, instead focusing on providing full-text content through license agreements.

Because the amount of books, journals, images, and other items that might be cataloged is so voluminous, they lend themselves to digitization, especially by large commercial publishers and vendors. EBSCO, Elsevier, ProQuest, Ovid, Oxford, Wiley, and other companies have invested millions of dollars into developing the computer systems necessary for indexing, abstracting, and creating full-text databases. To do so, they have negotiated agreements with hundreds of publishers to scan or upload journal content for current and back issues. Once they have aggregated hundreds of thousands to millions of articles, they sell licenses to the content to public, academic, special, and school libraries in a number of ways or "packages" such as the following:

- general titles across many broad subject disciplines;
- primary, secondary, and postsecondary grade levels;
- broad subject areas such as applied sciences, technology, the humanities and arts, the social sciences, the sciences, the environment, and so forth; and
- topics such as ethnic studies, library and information science, women's studies, education, book reviews, law, and so forth. The more specialized or topical full-text databases are particularly suited for large academic institutions with doctoral degrees or large programs such as environmental studies, law, gender studies, and so forth. Often, there may be some overlap in titles between or among the full-text databases that these large institutions license, but the vendors will negotiate prices to gain the sale.

School libraries at all levels are most interested in licensing full-text article databases that include general titles across many broad subject disciplines and that are appropriate for the grade levels of their students. The titles of the individual journal titles included in the full-text article database should ideally include the print titles that they currently subscribe to, or should be subscribing to, in order to support the curriculum.

Budgeting for virtual resources has become extremely important for individual school libraries unless the school district, state, or other entity provides access to them at no cost. If an individual school library must defray the entire cost of full-text and other database licenses, doing so can absorb a huge percentage of the budget. Vendors have tried many pricing models and even the same vendor can offer different options. One pricing model is to charge by the number of students enrolled. Some may charge by the seat or simultaneous user; libraries can add one or more seats until the right number is acquired so that "busy signals" are not encountered too often. Another model is to charge the equivalent of the library's print subscriptions, whether or not the library cancels the print subscriptions. That cost becomes the basis of its pricing for each subsequent year—with a provision for inflation, of course. In this case, the library's budget should not increase any more than it would if the library continued to pay the equivalent for the print subscriptions. Assuming that the use of the database will far surpass the use of the equivalent print resources, the cost of license is among the easiest to justify to school administrators. Other administrators might prefer buying only the number of seats required or which the budget can support. Because there is so much variability, the school librarian who has many licenses to monitor will spend a great deal of time tracking them.

The topical full-text database, on the other hand, is most likely to be used far less, so its cost will be harder to justify. This is especially true if there is a high percentage of overlap between the titles in the general and the topical databases. In many respects, the vendors' practice of repackaging journal content into small databases just to increase profits is abhorrent, particularly if it is designed to tap the library's materials budget needlessly. This seems to be obvious when a vendor is not willing to price the product by the number of seats, but instead charges by the number of students in the school or school district. In that case, the school may not wish to license a very specialized database because it might be used by debaters and honor students, but not the general student body. In any case, the annual cost of providing virtual resources has risen so fast in school libraries that such expenditures equal or surpass expenditures for all other sources of information.

No matter how these advances occurred at local, regional, or state levels, the vast majority of K–12 students today enjoy some degree of Internet access to databases licensed for their use.

Today, without multi-library licenses, few school libraries would have sufficient materials budgets to offer the wide array of full-text databases that they now enjoy. Thus the multi-library license agreements with database providers have become a fundamental part of today's information scene. The relationship has benefited both libraries and providers. The agreements have allowed libraries to stretch their materials budgets, while publishers and aggregators have realized new markets. This is particularly true when the individual libraries are free to cancel their print subscriptions. It should be noted, however, that vendors have been quick to put no-cancellation clauses in such multi-library license agreements.

Few might disagree that these changes in the information environment have been more revolutionary than evolutionary, given the pace at which they have occurred. Within literally a remarkable few years, access for K–12 students and teachers from any Internet-accessible workstation or laptop, in or outside of the school library, to a large array of full-text databases has become an expectation of taxpayers. This has been especially true when legislators in states as diverse as Maine, Alabama, Texas, and Ohio have provided funds to license products suitable for all state residents, including students in primary, secondary, and postsecondary institutions. The citizens of many states across the United States have benefited from this now widespread access to information and the journal literature. The authors surveyed the Web pages of many schools, school districts, and states across the United States and found an extensive list of databases made available to students and others. The most common online resources include the following:

General full-text periodicals (magazine/journal/newspaper)

- EBSCO: EBSCO Magazines, EBSCO Newspapers
- Gale Group (Thomson Gale): Academic ASAP, Expanded Academic ASAP, InfoTrac OneFile, General BusinessFile ASAP, General Reference Center Gold, Health Reference Center Academic, InfoTrac K–12 Kids Edition, InfoTrac K–12 Junior Edition. See galeschools.com for a detailed list.
- ProQuest: ProQuest Direct (national newspapers and journals)
- WilsonWeb Electronic Collection: Readers' Guide Full Text (Mega or Select Editions); Biography Reference Bank (combines Wilson Biographies Plus Illustrated and Biography Index with links to full-text articles, page images, and abstracts from the complete range of Wilson databases); plus others such as Famous First Facts, and many others aimed more to college libraries

Other

- ABC-CLIO Schools Social Studies Resources
- AccuNet/AP MultiMedia Archive
- AccuWeather
- ARTstor (digital images of art, architecture, sculpture, etc.)
- Columbia Encyclopedia
- Columbia International Affairs: CIAO
- CountryWatch
- CQ Researcher
- CQ Weekly Report
- Dictionary of Literary Biography
- eLibrary or Electric Library: Consumer-oriented magazines, books, newspapers, newswires, television and radio transcripts, photographs, and maps

- ERIC
- Familiar Quotations: A Collection of Passages, Phrases, and Proverbs Traced to Their Sources in Ancient and Modern Literature (Bartleby Library)
- Gale Group (Thomson Gale) offers more than seventy-five more specific or topical products, the most common of which included Biography Resource Center (includes content from Contemporary Authors), Contemporary Literary Criticism Select, Dictionary of Literary Biography, the Professional Collection, Criminal Justice Collection, Discovering Collection, InfoTrac Religion & Philosophy, Informe, Kids InfoBits, LitFinder, Newsletters ASAP, Pop Culture eCollection, Psychology eCollection, and Twayne's Authors Series
- Hoover's Business Network
- Information Please Almanac
- JSTOR Periodicals
- Kelly Blue Book
- Lands and Peoples
- LexisNexis Scholastic
- Merriam-Webster Online
- MLA International Bibliography
- netLibrary: Electronic books
- New Book of Knowledge Online (Grolier)
- NewsBank: Contemporary Newspapers
- Oxford Reference Online
- Peterson's College Database
- World Book Online
- WWWebster Dictionary and Thesaurus

In addition, most schools offer students access to federal, state, and local government information via links to the websites of those agencies.

- Interactive US Weather Map
- Medline
- National Weather Service
- US Patent Office
- and countless others

Readers can view brief descriptions of the above databases by using Google or a similar search engine. Because it is not the purpose of the authors to publish a reference guide to the sources, we leave it up to the reader to pursue descriptions of the above sources. It is also beyond the scope of this book to provide information to media specialists and other educators about how to teach information searching and retrieval skills. We have shown that K–12 students now access many millions of articles and documents when they have access to some of the full-text databases such as those listed above. It should be obvious that there are no media specialists, teachers, or school administrators who organize the articles or documents by their authoritativeness, accuracy, or any other attribute, of course. What educators can and should do, however, is provide students with the skills that allow them to sort through the content and critically evaluate the information they see on the Web.

A brief note on a leading general digital media resource for teachers, media specialists, school administrators, and students alike may be appropriate. Discovery Education offers a product called DigitalCurriculum. It provides curriculum on-demand videos, video clips, lesson plans, interactive assessments, encyclopedia content, still images, teacher modules and guides, lesson plans, and multimedia for most primary and secondary subjects. Used by millions of educators and students, it is an electronic resource that should be invaluable to school librarians, educators and administrators. The authors believe that it should encourage innovation as well as collaboration between media specialists, teachers, school administrators, and students. If the school library is to remain vital to the education of students, more collaboration on the curriculum is needed and such products as this might provide an additional conduit.

Despite all of the advantages they offer, school librarians should understand that there are reasons to be cautious. A few aggregators require the library to maintain print copies and require a surcharge for the electronic. Other license agreements require the libraries to continue paying the same amount as their print subscriptions, even if they are not renewed. Also, some providers want no-cancellation clauses—these should be avoided and be against school district, state, or other law. Similarly, some clauses require arbitration or legal proceedings to be on the vendor's or publisher's terms; this might also be against the law or district or governmental agency regulations. In such cases, it is always advisable for the school librarian to refer the agreement to the school administration or legal counsel. In the case of state or consortium-negotiated licenses, these clauses should have been examined and determined prior to asking individual libraries to sign the agreement (if required). Needless to say, acquiring books, tapes, DVDs and similar items is far less complicated.

Chapter Twenty-Three

Policy Components
for Virtual Resources

Many of the components of a collection development policy already discussed in previous chapters may be the same as those for virtual resources—but there are some decided differences. If this were not the case, the authors would not recommend writing a separate policy statement for virtual resources. This may be a separate part of a comprehensive policy, which makes it easy for the librarian to refer the reader to another section, rather than duplicating the same information. Sections that might very well be the same for physical and virtual products include the following:

- Mission
- Goals
- History of the library
- Teacher request process

There should be no need to repeat the information in these sections unless the policy on virtual resources is written to be a stand-alone statement. Either way, the uniqueness of many components relative to virtual resources requires a separate policy statement.

Some components of a policy statement covering virtual library resources such as licensing will be vastly different from those for physical library resources, particularly traditional materials such as books and audio or video items. In this chapter, we will focus on and discuss the following differences:

- Introduction to virtual resources
- Purpose of providing virtual resources
- Budgeting and funding of virtual resources

- License provisions and agreements
- Selection and evaluation criteria for virtual resources
- Deselection considerations
- Evaluation tools
- School district, consortial, and statewide licenses
- Additional resources

INTRODUCTION TO VIRTUAL RESOURCES

It is advisable to begin the policy statement with an introduction because most of the characteristics of virtual resources today are vastly different from those of physical resources. The introduction should provide the reader with the definition of virtual resources that the school library has adopted. A model definition might say that "virtual resources are the nonphysical databases that the library provides access to through the Internet."

Examples of virtual resources that the library licenses might also be included for clarity. For a virtual encyclopedia, for example, the statement might say that there are important differences from the print equivalent such as those appearing in the model statement below:

- With a print encyclopedia, what you see get is what you read. With a virtual encyclopedia, you can get what you read, plus what you hear, view, or link to. This is made possible if the publisher embeds hyperlinks in the text. For example:

  - The reader can click on a link to audio recordings such as speeches, songs, animal sounds, sound effects, and the like.
  - The reader can link to video clips such as ten second scenes from a film, a 3-D view of a building, a simulation, or a walk through an historic house or battle.
  - The reader can link to other entries within the encyclopedia or external to it such as words from a dictionary, books or articles cited by the author of the entry, etc.

- A virtual encyclopedia may be searched quite differently by the searcher using keyword or Boolean capabilities.
- The reader can download portions of the text to his or her own computer.

Other information that the librarian might want to include in the introduction is whether the library provides access to databases provided to it by the school district, a local or regional library or education consortium, or the state. If so, it bears mentioning that this is not true for physical resources.

PURPOSE OF PROVIDING VIRTUAL RESOURCES

This component of the policy should address the reasons why the library specifically wants to provide virtual resources. A common purpose included in many statements is "to provide greater and more convenient access to information for our users, including from home computer workstations, or other remote location." This emphasizes perhaps the most important difference from print resources, recognizing that virtual school library resources extend the reach of the library beyond its physical space on campus. A model example appears below and might be used to discuss the difference between a printed journal index and a full-text article database. Consider the statement as follows:

> The content of full-text article databases such as [name one or more licensed or accessible products] provides access to the articles in many journals as a result of database searches. The primary advantage of these virtual databases is that the student need only to click on the citation in order to view the article. A printed index to the periodical literature, on the other hand, provides citations to articles in journals that the library may or may not subscribe to. The student searching through a number of print indexes needs to note the citations, then determine if the library subscribes to the printed journal through our online catalog. The student then needs to locate the issue or bound volume of the journal s/he wants to examine and find the specific article in the volume. Failure to properly note the citation, lack of time, and finding articles razor-cut from the volume are all potential obstacles to finding the article. Virtual products, on the other hand, offer students nearly instantaneous access to the article, which is a click away using any PC that provides access to the Internet. There are also advantages to the school. The library, for instance, no longer needs to order individual subscriptions, send issues to a bindery, shelve and reshelve volumes, replace razor-cut articles, and shift volumes to make room for new ones. Such advantages of the full-text article database normally outweigh the cost of the license, provided the library cancels the print subscriptions to the journals whose article are included in the database.

It should be clear that students will benefit significantly if they can access the data anytime from home so long as they can log on to the Internet. This assumes, of course, that the school maintains a server with proper user authentication and verification protocols that meet the terms of the license agreement.

BUDGETING AND FUNDING OF VIRTUAL RESOURCES

Budget and funding considerations are unique for each school library in terms of dollar amounts, who must sign the licenses, whether the school is private or public, and a host of other variables. The school district or school principal, for instance, might require control over licensed databases for several reasons:

- Their high cost
- Computer and telecommunication considerations, including highly technical networking issues, user authentication and validation, technical staffing, and systems maintenance—all of which add to the cost of virtual resources
- Legal issues involved with licenses, particularly for city and county schools
- Cost-sharing issues (as when the school district requires apportionment of the costs among all or some schools)

For a normal book acquisition, there is a one-time cost. The selection or evaluation criteria and examples from a previous chapter should be applied. If a selection proved to be a poor one, there are only minor consequences because the cost is normally minor and nonrecurring.

This is generally never true when it comes to licensing virtual resources. The funding source of each virtual database is also important to consider. It is wise for the school librarian to assume that the cost of a virtual resource will be recurring as long as the database is used sufficiently to justify the annual cost.

It is generally not considered wise to plan on budgeting a full-text journal database for only one year, for instance, because students and teachers who learn to rely upon it will be upset if the license is not renewed. It may not even be advisable to invite all students and teachers to assess a trial of a full-text database with a vendor when the materials budget for the year is certain to be insufficient to cover its cost. The cost of a database license is invariably more costly in subsequent years. This is particularly true of full-text journal databases whose content grows every year by thousands of articles. Because such licenses are likely to consume a large percentage of the materials budget, a poor choice is generally costly. The public relations expense may also be costly, particularly if a number of people involved in the selection of the database is high. Naturally, more careful assessment of products, using the evaluation criteria suggested in previous chapters, would be prudent when all, or a major portion, of the funding must be allotted from the library's own materials budget. Consider the following:

- For a statewide database license whose cost is sustained by taxpayers and not the library, evaluation criteria are somewhat superfluous. Depending upon your viewpoint, there may be only one decision when it comes to providing access to a database that is provided at no cost the school library's budget: Do you provide a link to the "free" database or not?

- In such cases, a committee composed of librarians and educators from a variety of public, academic, and school libraries might have selected and negotiated a license with a vendor. The local school library is free to provide, or not provide, a link to that database with little consequence. It is assumed that there would be little likelihood for a public school not to provide a link to any grade appropriate database that was deemed appropriate for licensing under such circumstances.

LICENSE PROVISIONS AND AGREEMENTS

Except for shrink-wrapped computer software and some CD-ROMs or DVDs, librarians do not have to consider license agreements for other physical library resources. But virtual databases generally do come with license agreements and their terms are very important. License agreements must be signed by the responsible party for the institution and for the vendor. For school libraries, the responsible person is not normally the school librarian. The responsible party in schools may be the principal or school superintendent. The librarian, therefore, should not sign a license agreement unless he or she has been delegated the responsibility. This authority should be verifiable, for example, in a memorandum from the principal. The policy statement should address important provisions such as the following:

- The time period of the license. It is normally annual, but may be multiyear as well. If school policy prohibits multiyear agreements, the school librarian should make this known to the database provider and make certain the agreement is changed accordingly.
- Whether the database is licensed or a purchase and, in either case, whether annual maintenance fees apply.
- Whether the print subscription, when applicable, must continue to be subscribed to in order to have electronic access, or whether the print subscription may be cancelled with or without a discount or penalty. While librarians generally believe that electronic versions of a product should cost less than the print equivalent, most publishers and database providers do not share this.
- Who the authorized users are and who, therefore, the school's network or computer system's administrator must limit access to. Normally, all students and employees of the school are authorized users and should be given

access to the database if they can be authenticated and validated when they sign in to the school's network.

- Another important group of users for most libraries is the "walk-in." For the school library, the license should allow access for parents, trustees, volunteers, and others who might come to the library in search of information. Most vendors do allow database access for the walk-in.
- The license should state whether printing an article or document for a user at another, nonlicensed library is allowed or not. Any limitations for allowing interlibrary loans should be clearly stated in the agreement.
- The school is held harmless by the vendor from any action involving copyright, patent, and intellectual property claims. Conversely, the customer cannot indemnify the vendor against use of the database by the authorized database users.
- The jurisdiction where any suit must be filed for claims under the agreement. Other agreements will specify the use of an arbitrator because many governmental entities or laws prohibit adjudication elsewhere.
- Grounds for termination of the agreement by the vendor and licensee.
- Types and terms of license agreements

  - Individual workstation or single user license
  - Site license—only users who are physically in the school library or the building in which it is housed
  - Campus license—school students and employees located anywhere on school premises may connect their workstations or laptops to the database
  - School district license—school students and employees of the district may access the database, regardless of location (normally)
  - Statewide license—the state library or some other entity negotiated a license with the database provider allows any citizen of the state to access the database if they are authenticated and verified as an authorized user; for example, authorized users will be authenticated and verified by the school's, school district's, public library's, or academic institution's system or network
  - Consortium or other agency license—an educational or library group to which the school library or school district belongs may negotiate a license for its members

The policy might state that the preferred method of providing content to virtual resources is by means of multilibrary license agreements because their overall cost is normally significantly less than single library licenses. Providing the reader with at least one example may be helpful to illustrate the savings.

SELECTION AND EVALUATION
CRITERIA FOR VIRTUAL RESOURCES

For a normal book acquisition, there is a one-time decision based on the selection and evaluation criteria discussed in a previous chapter. A school librarian should base his or her decision regarding the selection of a virtual database on the same selection criteria he or she uses for selecting a book or audiovisual material as they apply. There is no reason, for example, to believe that evaluation criteria such as the accuracy and quality of the data, the authoritativeness of the authors, the reputation of the publisher, and the currency of information are any more or less important for a virtual database. In this chapter, therefore, the authors have chosen to focus only on the criteria that may be unique to virtual resources.

When it comes to evaluating electronic resources for the school library, there are many factors that might apply. If there is a choice between selecting an Internet accessible, virtual database, rather than a print or CD-ROM resource, the policy statement might address inherent advantages of the virtual resources such as the following:

a. Ability to use Boolean operators, keyword strategies, proximity searching, etc., to search text
b. Access by students outside the library from any Web-accessible computer
c. Access beyond regular library hours
d. Ability to download and print search results
e. Ability to link seamlessly to cited sources and reference tools

Compared to evaluating a single book written by one or two authors and published by one company, electronic journal databases may contain many thousands or millions of articles or documents from hundreds or thousands of journals that are written by as many or more authors and compiled by a vendor who negotiated rights from multiple publishers. A model statement headed "The Criteria for Virtual Resources" might say, for example:

> The selection and evaluation criteria for traditional library resources such as books [refer reader to the appropriate section of the policy] should apply to the content of virtual and all other library and information resources, regardless of how it is acquired, licensed, or accessed. However, there are some specific and unique criteria and advantages such as the following:
>
> - The database provider's interface is appropriate and easy to use.
> - The user of all our licensed databases has the ability to utilize a search engine provided by the database vendor; it will return specific content that matches keywords or descriptors the user enters.

- Many of our database providers offer links to images, film, or audio resources available on the Internet or from other databases that the library licenses.
- The user's ability to use the database in the school library where assistance is available or from the convenience of a home computer or laptop that provides Internet access. This advantage is available twenty-four hours a day, seven days a week unless the school's Internet server is unavailable to identify and verify the user of the licensed database.
- Because the content is located on the database provider's own content server in most instances, it may be updated frequently. Online sources generally, therefore, provide more up-to-date or current information than similar print titles. Mistakes or inaccuracies may also be corrected as soon as they are discovered. Books once published or films once produced, do not offer the ability to be instantly updated or corrected. It may be years until one edition of a book or film is updated.
- For some virtual databases, the vendor offers a way for the reader to easily navigate to related articles. For an encyclopedia, for example, the student no longer needs to locate another physical volume in a multivolume set, then find the specific page numbers cited in the original article, then try to photocopy the article. Rather, by clicking on a link to the article, access is instantaneous and the student can print the article, or a page from it, without leaving the computer.

If the database provider's interface is not appropriate and easy to use, there may be little reason to license the product despite all other advantages and qualities it may offer. For example, if the website for the product is so cluttered with information about the vendor, vendor products, contact information, specific database information, and so forth, that the student will exit the database without searching it, then the school librarian might offer the vendor this feedback and pursue licensing the product at a later time when the interface has improved. Today, this is not likely to be the case because vendors quickly learned just how essential a good interface is for users and paid dearly to hire the expertise needed to improve interfaces.

The statement might offer one or more examples. For instance, it might describe the difference between a printed encyclopedia and a virtual encyclopedia by the same publisher. For full-text journal databases, a parallel example may not be possible. Instead, the statement might use an example to point out some of the inherent advantages of full-text article databases as the following model statement suggests:

Full-text article databases offer students true content to the journal literature, not just citations to it, as do printed indexes. The articles are available almost instantly to the student who needs only to click on the citation from his Internet-accessible

PC. A list of journal titles included in virtual databases that are licensed by the library are generally the same ones that school librarians across the United States have had print subscriptions to for years and therefore have been evaluated carefully. Considering all the journal literature now available to our students through these full-text journal article databases, our students have access to unprecedented content.

The librarian might insert actual information about the number of print subscriptions once funded and the number of titles included in the full-text databases, excluding duplication (overlap titles), of course.

As is the case with books and audiovisual materials, content is one of the most important criteria for deciding whether to buy or license any virtual database. In evaluating virtual resources, the school librarian or selection and evaluation committee should assess the content of the database. A trial subscription is often employed to do so; most database providers are only too happy to provide a thirty-day trial. The school librarian should ask the network administrator to include a link to it from the school's website for everyone who might want to review it, or just for those selected by the librarian. For instance, the school librarian might want to invite only key teachers and administrators to provide feedback. This might be done by asking them to respond to questions such as the following:

- Is the content appropriate for the students it is intended for (i.e., is its scope appropriate for the grade level of the students)?
- Is the content (articles, documents, etc.) relevant to the curriculum?
- Is the format appropriate and cost-justified for the anticipated use?

With respect to the latter question, a book might be appropriate functioning as a very specialized, inexpensive reference source with an anticipated low-use; however, it would be far less appropriate—compared with a user license—for unlimited use. An unlimited user license, on the other hand, is entirely appropriate for content such as a general periodical database or general encyclopedia with an anticipated high remote and campus or in-house use. Content that frequently becomes out of date is an ideal candidate for a virtual database that is updated regularly. Articles in virtual encyclopedias or handbooks, for example, should be dated so as to allow librarians to assess their authoritativeness and accuracy.

If the librarian would decide against acquiring a book or film because the content was irrelevant to the curriculum or grade level of the students, the same criteria should guard against licensing or linking to a similar electronic resource. Even if access to a postsecondary electronic source such as Science Direct is provided through a state's virtual library, for instance, providing this specific link from an elementary or middle school library's homepage is not advisable because the journals are scholarly, peer reviewed titles appropriate for the postsecondary school market. The authors believe that a link to the state's virtual library website is advisable, but suggest that school librarians select only the specific links to products that are relevant to the grade levels of their students. This should not be considered a form of deselection because there is so much content available today, that school librarians must select only relevant links so as not to overwhelm students with "the world's literature."

DESELECTION CONSIDERATIONS

Due to cost, or cost per use, of virtual database licenses vis-à-vis library funds, deselection is a real consideration for licenses charged in whole or in part to the school library budget. The cost of full-text article databases is particularly vulnerable to increases because their content normally grows as the weekly, monthly, quarterly, or special issues of the journal titles are added to the database.

There is, however, another valid reason to cancel a license: cost per use. This consideration is more likely to be the case for a specialized database than a general one. The use of specialized databases is largely dependent on teacher assignments. Students may make little use of a play index if no teacher requires research assignments in that regard. By dividing the number of uses per month into the cost per month, we might get a cost that is many times the cost of a general literature, biography, or science full-text article database. Generally, students at all grade levels today will make high use of full-text article databases and low use of online journal indexes and abstracting sources.

Another reason for deselection may be that two virtual sources overlap in terms of content. If a statewide database becomes available at no cost to the library from a vendor, and it duplicates a similar database licensed and paid for from school library funds, it may be advisable to discontinue the latter license and use the savings for another product.

Database publishers and providers can change as a result of mergers and buyouts. Changes in personnel might also affect the quality and content of a virtual database. It is important, therefore, for school librarians to regularly evaluate databases and read reviews, or otherwise be vigilant for news that might impact the quality of database content. If the staff of a publisher is cut, for instance, the database content may not be updated as frequently as once was the case. If the library can acquire the competing product for the same or less money and all other variables are the same, it may be time for a switch. Or, if the competing product is available through a statewide database, the librarian can provide the link from the library's website and notify the vendor to cancel the license at the end of the agreement.

EVALUATION TOOLS

Specialized and unique tools are available to school librarians who wish to read what reviewers have to say about specific virtual resources. Given the initial and annual licensing cost of most licenses, reading one or more reviews cannot be encouraged enough, particularly when the library's own budget is the source of funding. The date of the review is highly important because most providers make frequent changes in response to criticism of their product. If the date is not provided, the authors suggest that the school librarian examine the database to determine if the criticism is still valid.

The Charleston Advisor, www.charlestonco.com/

ChoiceReviews.online, www.ala.org/ala/acrl/acrlpubs/choice/choicereviews/
    ChoiceReviews_online.htm

Fulltext Sources Online, www.fso-online.com/

Gale Directory of Databases, http://library.dialog.com/bluesheets/html/
    bl0230.html

KidsClick! www.kidsclick.com

Librarians' Internet Index (LII), http://lii.org/

Library Journal, www.libraryjournal.com/ (click "Reviews")

H. W. Wilson, www.hwwilson.com/reviews/databasereviews.htm

SCHOOL DISTRICT, CONSORTIAL, AND STATEWIDE LICENSES

The policy should state what memberships, partnerships, or relationships it has that might have an impact on what virtual resources the library might be able to offer users. For example, if the school is only one of several high school libraries in a large school district or consortia, this information should be included. Briefly stating how the library benefits in terms of database licenses is appropriate. Examples are always helpful. This is even more true of state and multistate database agreements. If statewide database licenses are paid for from taxes, including published information or a website (URL) will also be helpful.

ADDITIONAL RESOURCES

The reader should see Jane Pearlmutter's chapter in *Library Collection Development Policies: Academic, Public, and Special Libraries* (Scarecrow Press, 1995), pp. 218–29. She cites a number of articles that discuss potentially useful websites. Also, Chapter 29, "Discussion of Recent Issues," pp. 230–42, will provide additional insight into the nature of virtual resources.

Appendix A

Institutions Contributing Policy Excerpts

Note: In cases where the web addresses have been changed or no longer function properly, search the URL in the Wayback Machine, located at www.archive.org.

Aldine Independent School District Library Media Services Department. 14910 Aldine Westfield Road, Houston, TX 77032. 281-449-1011. www.aldine.k12.tx.us.

Alemany High School Library. 11111 Alemany Drive, Mission Hills, CA 91345. 818-365-3925/Ext. 238. M. Michele Brown Kiske, Librarian.

Apponequet Regional High School Library. Freetown-Lakeville Regional School District, 100 Howland District, Lakeville, MA 02347. 508-947-2660/Ext. 1136. Irene Ashley, Ext. 1192. http://users.rcn.com/libra/index.html.

Atwater Elementary School District. 1401 Broadway Avenue, Atwater, CA 95301. 209-357-6100. http://mse.aesd.k12.ca.us/library/selectpol.html.

Baltimore County Public Schools. Department of Curriculum and Instruction, 6901 Charles Street, Towson, MD 21204. www.beps.org/offices/lis/office/admin/selection.html.

Bowling Green City School District. http://winslo.state.oh.us/publib/material-bg.html.

Calgary Board of Education, 515 Macleod Trail S.E., Calgard, AB, Canada T2G 2L9. http://cbe.ab.ca.

Chico Unified School District. Professional Library, 1163 E. 7th Street, Chico, CA 95926. 530-879-5197. www.cusd.chico.k12.ca.us/.

Delaware Valley School District. 236 Rte. 6 & 209, Milford, PA 18337. 570-296-1800. http://dvasdweb.dvasd.k12.pa.us/.

Edmonton Public Schools. One Kingsway, Edmonton, Alberta, Canada TSH 4G9. 780-429-8000. www.epsb.ca/index.shtml. info@epsb.ca.

Education Service Center, Region 2, 209 North Water Street, Corpus Christi, TX 78401-2599. 361-561-8400; 361-883-3442 (fax).

Groton Public Schools, Media Technology Services. 1300 Flanders Road, Mystic, CT 06355. 860-572-2100. www.groton.k12.ct.us/centraloffice/mts.html.

Hawaii Department of Education, Office of Instructional Services, School Library Services. 475 22nd Avenue, Bldg. 302, Room 203, Honolulu, HI 96816. 808-733-9150. Lucretia Leong, SLS Specialist III, luleong@k12.hi.us. http://sls.k12.hi.us/selection.html.

Longview Independent School District. 1301 E. Young Street, Longview, TX 75602. 903-381-2200.

Los Angeles Unified School District. 333 S. Beaudry Avenue, Los Angeles, CA 90017. 213-241-1000. lausdk12.ca.us.

Mt. Ararat High School. 73 Eagles Way, Topsham, ME 04086. 207-729-2951. www.mta75.org/library/selectionpolicy.html.

Norman Public Schools Library. 131 S. Flood Avenue, Norman, OK 73069. 405-364-1339. www.norman.k12.ok.us/.

Northeast Community School District. 1450 370th Avenue, Goose Lake, IA 52750. 563-577-2249. www.iema-ia.org/IEMA101.html.

Nueva School, Library. 6565 Skyline Boulevard, Hillsborough, CA 94010. 650-348-2272. www.khsd.k12.ca.us/nueva/.

Red Deer Public School District, Alberta, Canada. www.rdpsd.ab.ca.

Rogers Public School System. 212 S. 3rd Street, Rogers, AR 72756. 479-636-3910. www.rogers.k12.ar.us/users/mcook/selection.html.

Saskatoon Public School Division, Saskatchewan, Canada. www.sbe.saskatoon.sk.ca.

Scecina Memorial High School. 5000 Nowland Avenue, Indianapolis, IN 46201. 317-356-6377. www.scecina.org/.

School District of Philadelphia. 440 North Broad Street, Philadelphia, PA 19130. 215-400-4170. www.philsch.k12.pa.us/.

Squires Elementary School Library. 3337 Squire Oak Drive, Lexington, KY 40515. 859-381-3002. Lisa Pollock, Media Specialist. www.squires.fcps.net/library/

St. Joseph School, Library. 700 18th Avenue E, Seattle, WA 98112. 206-329-3260. www.stjosephsea.org/.

University Laboratory High School, Library, 1212 W. Springfield, Urbana, IL 61801. 217-333-1589. Frances Jacobson Harris, Librarian. www.uni.uiuc.edu/library/policies/collectiondevelopment.html.

Wilmington School District. 211 Route 9 West, Wilmington, VT 05363. 802-464-1300. www.dves.k12.vt.us/Users/cethier/libpol.html.

Appendix B

Intellectual Freedom
Statements and Forms

Intellectual freedom statements and forms include the following:

- Access for Children and Young Adults to Nonprint Materials
- Access to Electronic Information, Services, and Networks
- Access to Library Resources and Services Regardless of Sex, Gender Identity, or Sexual Orientation
- Challenged Materials
- Dealing with Concerns about Library Resources
- Diversity in Collection Development
- Economic Barriers to Information Access
- Evaluating Library Collections
- Exhibit Spaces and Bulletin Boards
- Expurgation of Library Materials
- Free Access to Libraries for Minors
- The Freedom to Read Statement
- The Freedom to View Statement
- Guidelines for the Development and Implementation of Policies, Regulations and Procedures Affecting Access to Library Materials, Services and Facilities
- Guidelines for the Development of Policies and Procedures
- Regarding User Behavior and Library Usage
- Library Bill of Rights
- Library-Initiated Programs as a Resource
- Policy concerning Confidentiality of Personally Identifiable Information about Library Users
- Policy on Governmental Intimidation
- Resolution on Access to the Use of Libraries and Information by Individuals with Physical or Mental Impairment

- Resolution on the Use of Filtering Software in Libraries
- Restricted Access to Library Materials
- Statement on Labeling
- The Universal Right to Free Expression

ACCESS TO ELECTRONIC INFORMATION, SERVICES, AND NETWORKS: AN INTERPRETATION OF THE LIBRARY BILL OF RIGHTS

The world is in the midst of an electronic communications revolution. Based on its constitutional, ethical, and historical heritage, American librarianship is uniquely positioned to address the broad range of information issues being raised in this revolution. In particular, librarians address intellectual freedom from a strong ethical base and an abiding commitment to the preservation of the individual's rights.

Freedom of expression is an inalienable human right and the foundation for self-government. Freedom of expression encompasses the freedom of speech and the corollary right to receive information. These rights extend to minors as well as adults. Libraries and librarians exist to facilitate the exercise of these rights by selecting, producing, providing access to, identifying, retrieving, organizing, providing instruction in the use of, and preserving recorded expression regardless of the format or technology.

The American Library Association expresses these basic principles of librarianship in its *Code of Ethics* and in the *Library Bill of Rights* and its Interpretations. These serve to guide librarians and library governing bodies in addressing issues of intellectual freedom that arise when the library provides access to electronic information, services, and networks.

Issues arising from the still-developing technology of computer-mediated information generation, distribution, and retrieval need to be approached and regularly reviewed from a context of constitutional principles and ALA policies so that fundamental and traditional tenets of librarianship are not swept away.

Electronic information flows across boundaries and barriers despite attempts by individuals, governments, and private entities to channel or control it. Even so, many people, for reasons of technology, infrastructure, or socioeconomic status do not have access to electronic information.

In making decisions about how to offer access to electronic information, each library should consider its mission, goals, objectives, cooperative agreements, and the needs of the entire community it serves.

The Rights of Users

All library system and network policies, procedures or regulations relating to electronic resources and services should be scrutinized for potential violation of user rights.

User policies should be developed according to the policies and guidelines established by the American Library Association, including *Guidelines for the Development and Implementation of Policies, Regulations, and Procedures Affecting Access to Library Materials, Services and Facilities.*

Users should not be restricted or denied access for expressing or receiving constitutionally protected speech. Users' access should not be changed without due process, including, but not limited to, formal notice and a means of appeal.

Although electronic systems may include distinct property rights and security concerns, such elements may not be employed as a subterfuge to deny users' access to information. Users have the right to be free of unreasonable limitations or conditions set by libraries, librarians, system administrators, vendors, network service providers, or others. Contracts, agreements, and licenses entered into by libraries on behalf of their users should not violate this right. Users also have a right to information, training and assistance necessary to operate the hardware and software provided by the library.

Users have both the right of confidentiality and the right of privacy. The library should uphold these rights by policy, procedure, and practice. Users should be advised, however, that because security is technically difficult to achieve, electronic transactions and files could become public. The rights of users who are minors shall in no way be abridged.[1]

Equity of Access

Electronic information, services, and networks provided directly or indirectly by the library should be equally, readily and equitably accessible to all library users. American Library Association policies oppose the charging of user fees for the provision of information services by all libraries and information services that receive their major support from public funds (50.3; 53.1.14; 60.1; 61.1). It should be the goal of all libraries to develop policies concerning access to electronic resources in light of *Economic Barriers to Information Access: An Interpretation of the Library Bill of Rights* and *Guidelines for the Development and Implementation of Policies, Regulations and Procedures Affecting Access to Library Materials, Services and Facilities.*

Information Resources and Access

Providing connections to global information, services, and networks is not the same as selecting and purchasing material for a library collection. Determining the accuracy or authenticity of electronic information may present special problems. Some information accessed electronically may not meet a library's selection or collection development policy. It is, therefore, left to each user to determine what is appropriate. Parents and legal guardians who are concerned about their children's use of electronic resources should provide guidance to their own children.

Libraries and librarians should not deny or limit access to information available via electronic resources because of its allegedly controversial content or because of the librarian's personal beliefs or fear of confrontation. Information retrieved or utilized electronically should be considered constitutionally protected unless determined otherwise by a court with appropriate jurisdiction.

Libraries, acting within their mission and objectives, must support access to information on all subjects that serve the needs or interests of each user, regardless of the user's age or the content of the material. Libraries have an obligation to provide access to government information available in electronic format. Libraries and librarians should not deny access to information solely on the grounds that it is perceived to lack value.

In order to prevent the loss of information, and to preserve the cultural record, libraries may need to expand their selection or collection development policies to ensure preservation, in appropriate formats, of information obtained electronically.

Electronic resources provide unprecedented opportunities to expand the scope of information available to users. Libraries and librarians should provide access to information presenting all points of view. The provision of access does not imply sponsorship or endorsement. These principles pertain to electronic resources no less than they do to the more traditional sources of information in libraries.[2]

[Adopted by the ALA Council, January 24, 1996]

ACCESS FOR CHILDREN AND YOUNG ADULTS TO NONPRINT MATERIALS: AN INTERPRETATION OF THE LIBRARY BILL OF RIGHTS

Library collections of nonprint materials raise a number of intellectual freedom issues, especially regarding minors. Article V of the *Library Bill of Rights* states, "A person's right to use a library should not be denied or abridged because of origin, age, background, or views."

The American Library Association's principles protect minors' access to sound, images, data, games, software, and other content in all formats such as tapes, CDs, DVDs, music CDs, computer games, software, databases, and other emerging technologies. ALA's *Free Access to Libraries for Minors: An Interpretation of the Library Bill of Rights* states,

> The "right to use a library" includes free access to, and unrestricted use of, all the services, materials, and facilities the library has to offer. Every restriction on access to, and use of, library resources, based solely on the chronological age, educational level, literacy skills, or legal emancipation of users violates Article V. . . .
>
> [P]arents—and only parents—have the right and responsibility to restrict access of their children—and only their children—to library resources. Parents who do not want their children to have access to certain library services, materials, or facilities should so advise their children. Librarians and library governing bodies cannot assume the role of parents or the functions of parental authority in the private relationship between parent and child.

Lack of access to information can be harmful to minors. Librarians and library governing bodies have a public and professional obligation to ensure that all members of the community they serve have free, equal, and equitable access to the entire range of library resources regardless of content, approach, format, or amount of detail. This principle of library service applies equally to all users, minors as well as adults. Librarians and library governing bodies must uphold this principle in order to provide adequate and effective service to minors.

Policies that set minimum age limits for access to any nonprint materials or information technology, with or without parental permission, abridge library use for minors. Age limits based on the cost of the materials are also unacceptable. Librarians, when dealing with minors, should apply the same standards to circulation of nonprint materials as are applied to books and other print materials except when directly and specifically prohibited by law.

Recognizing that librarians cannot act *in loco parentis*, ALA acknowledges and supports the exercise by parents of their responsibility to guide their own children's reading and viewing. Libraries should provide published reviews and/or reference works that contain information about the content, subject matter, and recommended audiences for nonprint materials. These resources will assist parents in guiding their children without implicating the library in censorship.

In some cases, commercial content ratings, such as the *Motion Picture Association of America* (MPAA) movie ratings, might appear on the packaging or promotional materials provided by producers or distributors. However, marking out or removing this information from materials or packaging constitutes expurgation or censorship.

MPAA movie ratings, *Entertainment Software Rating Board* (ESRB) game ratings, and other rating services are private advisory codes and have no legal standing (*Expurgation of Library Materials*). For the library to add ratings to nonprint materials if they are not already there is unacceptable. It is also unacceptable to post a list of such ratings with a collection or to use them in circulation policies or other procedures. These uses constitute labeling, "an attempt to prejudice attitudes" (*Statement on Labeling*), and are forms of censorship. The application of locally generated ratings schemes intended to provide content warnings to library users is also inconsistent with the Library Bill of Rights.

The interests of young people, like those of adults, are not limited by subject, theme, or level of sophistication. Librarians have a responsibility to ensure young people's access to materials and services that reflect diversity of content and format sufficient to meet their needs.

[Adopted June 28, 1989, by the ALA Council; the quotation from *Free Access to Libraries for Minors* was changed after Council adopted the July 3, 1991, and the June 30, 2004, revision of that *Interpretation*; amended June 30, 2004, by the ALA Council]

ACCESS TO LIBRARY RESOURCES AND SERVICES REGARDLESS OF SEX, GENDER IDENTITY, OR SEXUAL ORIENTATION: AN INTERPRETATION OF THE LIBRARY BILL OF RIGHTS

American libraries exist and function within the context of a body of laws derived from the United States Constitution and the *First Amendment*. The *Library Bill of Rights* embodies the basic policies which guide libraries in the provision of services, materials, and programs.

In the preamble to its *Library Bill of Rights*, the American Library Association affirms that *all* [emphasis added] libraries are forums for information and ideas. This concept of *forum* and its accompanying principle of *inclusiveness* pervade all six Articles of the *Library Bill of Rights*.

The American Library Association stringently and unequivocally maintains that libraries and librarians have an obligation to resist efforts that systematically exclude materials dealing with any subject matter, including sex, gender identity, or sexual orientation:

- Article I of the *Library Bill of Rights* states that "[m]aterials should not be excluded because of the origin, background, or views of those contributing to their creation." The Association affirms that books and other materials coming from gay, lesbian, bisexual, and/or transgendered presses, gay, lesbian, bisexual and/or transgendered authors or other creators, and materials regardless of format or services dealing with gay, lesbian, bisexual and/or transgendered life are protected by the *Library Bill of Rights*. Librarians are obligated by the *Library Bill of Rights* to endeavor to select materials without regard to the sex, gender identity, or sexual orientation of their creators by using the criteria identified in their written, approved selection policies (*ALA policy 53.1.5*).

- Article II maintains that "[l]ibraries should provide materials and information presenting all points of view on current and historical issues. Materials should not be proscribed or removed because of partisan or doctrinal disapproval." Library services, materials, and programs representing diverse points of view on sex, gender identity, or sexual orientation should be considered for purchase and inclusion in library collections and programs (ALA policies *53.1.1*, *53.1.9*, and *53.1.11*). The Association affirms that attempts to proscribe or remove materials dealing with gay, lesbian, bisexual, and/or transgendered life without regard to the written, approved selection policy violate this tenet and constitute censorship.
- Articles III and IV mandate that libraries "challenge censorship" and cooperate with those "resisting abridgement of free expression and free access to ideas."
- Article V holds that "[a] person's right to use a library should not be denied or abridged because of origin, age, background or views." In the *Library Bill of Rights* and all its Interpretations, it is intended that "origin" encompasses all the characteristics of individuals that are inherent in the circumstances of their birth; "age" encompasses all the characteristics of individuals that are inherent in their levels of development and maturity; "background" encompasses all the characteristics of individuals that are a result of their life experiences; and "views" encompasses all the opinions and beliefs held and expressed by individuals. Therefore, Article V of the *Library Bill of Rights* mandates that library services, materials, and programs be available to all members of the community the library serves, without regard to sex, gender identity, or sexual orientation. This includes providing youth with comprehensive sex education literature (*ALA Policy 52.5.2*).
- Article VI maintains that "[l]ibraries which make exhibit spaces and meeting rooms available to the public they serve should make such facilities available on an equitable basis, regardless of the beliefs or affiliations of individuals or groups requesting their use." This protection extends to all groups and members of the community the library serves, without regard to sex, gender identity, or sexual orientation.

The American Library Association holds that any attempt, be it legal or extra-legal, to regulate or suppress library services, materials, or programs must be resisted in order that protected expression is not abridged. Librarians have a professional obligation to ensure that all library users have free and equal access to the entire range of library services, materials, and programs. Therefore, the Association strongly opposes any effort to limit access to information and ideas. The Association also encourages librarians to proactively support the First Amendment rights of all library users, regardless of sex, gender identity, or sexual orientation.

[Adopted June 30, 1993; amended July 12, 2000, by the ALA Council; amended June 30, 2004, by the ALA Council]

CHALLENGED MATERIALS:
AN INTERPRETATION OF THE LIBRARY BILL OF RIGHTS

The American Library Association declares as a matter of firm principle that it is the responsibility of every library to have a clearly defined materials selection policy in written form that reflects the *Library Bill of Rights*, and that is approved by the appropriate governing authority.

Challenged materials that meet the criteria for selection in the materials selection policy of the library should not be removed under any legal or extra-legal pressure. The *Library Bill of Rights* states in Article I that "[m]aterials should not be excluded because of the origin, background, or views of those contributing to their creation," and in Article II, that "[m]aterials should not be proscribed or removed because of partisan or doctrinal disapproval." Freedom of expression is protected by the Constitution of the United States, but constitutionally protected expression is often separated from unprotected expression only by a dim and uncertain line. The Constitution requires a procedure designed to focus searchingly on challenged expression before it can be suppressed. An adversary hearing is a part of this procedure.

Therefore, any attempt, be it legal or extra-legal, to regulate or suppress materials in libraries must be closely scrutinized to the end that protected expression is not abridged.

[Adopted June 25, 1971; amended July 1, 1981; amended January 10, 1990, by the ALA Council]

DEALING WITH CONCERNS
ABOUT LIBRARY RESOURCES

As with any public service, libraries receive complaints and expressions of concern. One of the librarian's responsibilities is to handle these complaints in a respectful and fair manner. The complaints that librarians often worry about most are those dealing with library resources or free access policies. The key to successfully handling these complaints is to be sure the library staff and the governing authorities are all knowledgeable about the complaint procedures and their implementation. As normal operating procedure, each library should:

1. *Maintain a materials selection policy.* It should be in written form and approved by the appropriate governing authority. It should apply to all library materials equally.
2. *Maintain a library service policy.* This should cover registration policies, programming, and services in the library that involve access issues.
3. *Maintain a clearly defined method for handling complaints.* The complaint must be filed in writing and the complainant must be properly identified before action is taken. A decision should be deferred until fully considered by appropriate administrative authority. The process should be followed, whether the complaint originates internally or externally.
4. *Maintain in-service training.* Conduct periodic in-service training to acquaint staff, administration, and the governing authority with the materials selection policy and library service policy and procedures for handling complaints.
5. *Maintain lines of communication with civic, religious, educational, and political bodies of the community.* Library board and staff participation in local civic organizations and presentations to these organizations should emphasize the library's selection process and intellectual freedom principles.
6. *Maintain a vigorous public information program on behalf of intellectual freedom.* Newspapers, radio, and television should be informed of policies governing resource selection and use, and of any special activities pertaining to intellectual freedom.
7. *Maintain familiarity with any local, municipal, and state legislation pertaining to intellectual freedom and First Amendment rights.* Following these practices will not preclude receiving complaints from pressure groups or individuals but should provide a base from which to operate when these concerns are expressed. When a complaint is made, follow one or more of the steps listed below:

   a. Listen calmly and courteously to the complaint. Remember the person has a right to express a concern. Use of good communication skills helps many people understand the need for diversity in library collections and the use of library resources. In the event the person is not satisfied, advise the complainant of the library policy and procedures for handling library resource statements of concern. If a person does fill out a form about their concern, make sure a prompt written reply related to the concern is sent.

b. It is essential to notify the administration and/or the governing authority (library board, etc.) of the complaint and assure them that the library's procedures are being followed. Present full, written information giving the nature of the complaint and identifying the source.

c. When appropriate, seek the support of the local media. Freedom to read and freedom of the press go hand in hand.

d. When appropriate, inform local civic organizations of the facts and enlist their support. Meet negative pressure with positive pressure.

e. Assert the principles of the *Library Bill of Rights* as a professional responsibility. Laws governing obscenity, subversive material and other questionable matter are subject to interpretation by courts. Library resources found to meet the standards set in the materials selection or collection development policy should not be removed or restricted from public access until after an adversary hearing resulting in a final judicial determination.

f. Contact the *ALA Office for Intellectual Freedom* and your *state intellectual freedom committee* to inform them of the complaint and to enlist their support and the assistance of other agencies.

The principles and procedures discussed above apply to all kinds of resource related complaints or attempts to censor and are supported by groups such as the National Education Association, the American Civil Liberties Union, and the National Council of Teachers of English, as well as the American Library Association. While the practices provide positive means for preparing for and meeting pressure group complaints, they serve the more general purpose of supporting the *Library Bill of Rights*, particularly Article 3, which states that "[l]ibraries should challenge censorship in the fulfillment of the responsibility to provide information and enlightenment."

Office for Intellectual Freedom
American Library Association
50 E. Huron Street
Chicago, IL 60611
312/280-4223
oif@ala.org

[Revised by the Intellectual Freedom Committee, January 12, 1983; November 17, 2000]

DIVERSITY IN COLLECTION DEVELOPMENT:
AN INTERPRETATION OF THE LIBRARY BILL OF RIGHTS

Throughout history, the focus of censorship has fluctuated from generation to generation. Books and other materials have not been selected or have been removed from library collections for many reasons, among which are prejudicial language and ideas, political content, economic theory, social philosophies, religious beliefs, sexual forms of expression, and other potentially controversial topics.

Some examples of censorship may include removing or not selecting materials because they are considered by some as racist or sexist; not purchasing conservative religious materials; not selecting materials about or by minorities because it is thought these groups or interests are not represented in a community; or not providing information on or materials from non-mainstream political entities.

Librarians may seek to increase user awareness of materials on various social concerns by many means, including, but not limited to, issuing bibliographies and presenting exhibits and programs. Librarians have a professional responsibility to be inclusive, not exclusive, in collection development and in the provision of interlibrary loan. Access to all materials legally obtainable should be assured to the user, and policies should not unjustly exclude materials even if they are offensive to the librarian or the user. Collection development should reflect the philosophy inherent in Article II of *the Library Bill of Rights*: "Libraries should provide materials and information presenting all points of view on current and historical issues. Materials should not be proscribed or removed because of partisan or doctrinal disapproval." A balanced collection reflects a diversity of materials, not an equality of numbers. Collection development responsibilities include selecting materials in the languages in common use in the community the library serves. Collection development and the selection of materials should be done according to professional standards and established selection and review procedures.

There are many complex facets to any issue, and variations of context in which issues may be expressed, discussed, or interpreted. Librarians have a professional responsibility to be fair, just, and equitable and to give all library users equal protection in guarding against violation of the library patron's right to read, view, or listen to materials and resources protected by the *First Amendment*, no matter what the viewpoint of the author, creator, or selector. Librarians have an obligation to protect library collections from removal of materials based on personal bias or prejudice, and to select and support the access to materials on all subjects that meet, as closely as possible, the needs, interests, and abilities of all persons in the community the library serves. This includes materials that reflect political, economic, religious, social, minority, and sexual issues.

Intellectual freedom, the essence of equitable library services, provides for free access to all expressions of ideas through which any and all sides of a question, cause, or movement may be explored. Toleration is meaningless without tolerance for what some may consider detestable. Librarians cannot justly permit their own preferences to limit their degree of tolerance in collection development, because freedom is indivisible.

[Adopted July 14, 1982; amended January 10, 1990, by the ALA Council]

ECONOMIC BARRIERS TO INFORMATION ACCESS: AN INTERPRETATION OF THE LIBRARY BILL OF RIGHTS

A democracy presupposes an informed citizenry. The *First Amendment* mandates the right of all persons to free expression, and the corollary right to receive the constitutionally protected expression of others. The publicly supported library provides free, equal, and equitable access to information for all people of the community the library serves. While the roles, goals, and objectives of publicly supported libraries may differ, they share this common mission.

The library's essential mission must remain the first consideration for librarians and governing bodies faced with economic pressures and competition for funding.

In support of this mission, the American Library Association has enumerated certain principles of library services in the *Library Bill of Rights*.

Principles Governing Fines, Fees, and User Charges

Article I of the *Library Bill of Rights* states,

> Books and other library resources should be provided for the interest, information, and enlightenment of all people of the community the library serves.

Article V of the *Library Bill of Rights* states,

> A person's right to use a library should not be denied or abridged because of origin, age, background, or views.

The American Library Association opposes the charging of user fees for the provision of information by all libraries and information services that receive their major support from public funds. All information resources that are provided directly or indirectly by the library, regardless of technology, format, or methods of delivery, should be readily, equally and equitably accessible to all library users.

Libraries that adhere to these principles systematically monitor their programs of service for potential barriers to access and strive to eliminate such barriers when they occur. All library policies and procedures, particularly those involving fines, fees, or other user charges, should be scrutinized for potential barriers to access. All services should be designed and implemented with care, so as not to infringe on or interfere with the provision or delivery of information and resources for all users. Services should be reevaluated regularly to ensure that the library's basic mission remains uncompromised.

Librarians and governing bodies should look for alternative models and methods of library administration that minimize distinctions among users based on their economic status or financial condition. They should resist the temptation to impose user fees to alleviate financial pressures, at long-term cost to institutional integrity and public confidence in libraries.

Library services that involve the provision of information, regardless of format, technology, or method of delivery, should be made available to all library users on an equal and equitable basis. Charging fees for the use of library collections, services, programs, or facilities that were purchased with public funds raises barriers to access. Such fees effectively abridge or deny access for some members of the community because they reinforce distinctions among users based on their ability and willingness to pay.

Principles Governing Conditions of Funding

Article II of the *Library Bill of Rights* states,

> Materials should not be proscribed or removed because of partisan or doctrinal disapproval.

Article III of the *Library Bill of Rights* states,

> Libraries should challenge censorship in the fulfillment of their responsibility to provide information and enlightenment.

Article IV of the *Library Bill of Rights* states,

> Libraries should cooperate with all persons and groups concerned with resisting abridgment of free expression and free access to ideas.

The American Library Association opposes any legislative or regulatory attempt to impose content restrictions on library resources, or to limit user access to information, as a condition of funding for publicly supported libraries and information services.

The First Amendment guarantee of freedom of expression is violated when the right to receive that expression is subject to arbitrary restrictions based on content.

Librarians and governing bodies should examine carefully any terms or conditions attached to library funding and should oppose attempts to limit through such conditions full and equal access to information because of content. This principle applies equally to private gifts or bequests and to public funds. In particular, librarians and governing bodies have an obligation to reject such restrictions when the effect of the restriction is to limit equal and equitable access to information.

Librarians and governing bodies should cooperate with all efforts to create a community consensus that publicly supported libraries require funding unfettered by restrictions. Such a consensus supports the library mission to provide the free and unrestricted exchange of information and ideas necessary to a functioning democracy.

The Association's historic position in this regard is stated clearly in a number of Association policies: 50.4 "Free Access to Information," 50.8 "Financing of Libraries," 51.2 "Equal Access to Library Service," 51.3 "Intellectual Freedom," 53 "Intellectual Freedom Policies," 59.1 "Policy Objectives," and 60 "Library Services for the Poor."
[Adopted by the ALA Council, June 30, 1993]

EVALUATING LIBRARY COLLECTIONS:
AN INTERPRETATION OF THE LIBRARY BILL OF RIGHTS

The continuous review of library materials is necessary as a means of maintaining an active library collection of current interest to users. In the process, materials may be added and physically deteriorated or obsolete materials may be replaced or removed in accordance with the collection maintenance policy of a given library and the needs of the community it serves. Continued evaluation is closely related to the goals and responsibilities of all libraries and is a valuable tool of collection development. This procedure is not to be used as a convenient means to remove materials presumed to be controversial or disapproved of by segments of the community. Such abuse of the evaluation function violates the principles of intellectual freedom and is in opposition to the Preamble and Articles I and II of the *Library Bill of Rights*, which state,

> The American Library Association affirms that all libraries are forums for information and ideas, and that the following basic policies should guide their services.

I. Books and other library resources should be provided for the interest, information, and enlightenment of all people of the community the library serves. Materials should not be excluded because of the origin, background, or views of those contributing to their creation.

II. Libraries should provide materials and information presenting all points of view on current and historical issues. Materials should not be proscribed or removed because of partisan or doctrinal disapproval.

The American Library Association opposes such "silent censorship" and strongly urges that libraries adopt guidelines setting forth the positive purposes and principles of evaluation of materials in library collections. [Adopted February 2, 1973; amended July 1, 1981, by the ALA Council]

EXHIBIT SPACES AND BULLETIN BOARDS: AN INTERPRETATION OF THE LIBRARY BILL OF RIGHTS

Libraries often provide exhibit spaces and bulletin boards. The uses made of these spaces should conform to the *Library Bill of Rights*: Article I states, "Materials should not be excluded because of the origin, background, or views of those contributing to their creation." Article II states, "Materials should not be proscribed or removed because of partisan or doctrinal disapproval." Article VI maintains that exhibit space should be made available "on an equitable basis, regardless of the beliefs or affiliations of individuals or groups requesting their use."

In developing library exhibits, staff members should endeavor to present a broad spectrum of opinion and a variety of viewpoints. Libraries should not shrink from developing exhibits because of controversial content or because of the beliefs or affiliations of those whose work is represented. Just as libraries do not endorse the viewpoints of those whose work is represented in their collections, libraries also do not endorse the beliefs or viewpoints of topics that may be the subject of library exhibits.

Exhibit areas often are made available for use by community groups. Libraries should formulate a written policy for the use of these exhibit areas to assure that space is provided on an equitable basis to all groups that request it.

Written policies for exhibit space use should be stated in inclusive rather than exclusive terms. For example, a policy that the library's exhibit space is open "to organizations engaged in educational, cultural, intellectual, or charitable activities" is an inclusive statement of the limited uses of the exhibit space. This defined limitation would permit religious groups to use the exhibit space because they engage in intellectual activities, but would exclude most commercial uses of the exhibit space.

A publicly supported library may designate use of exhibit space for strictly library-related activities, provided that this limitation is viewpoint neutral and clearly defined.

Libraries may include in this policy rules regarding the time, place, and manner of use of the exhibit space, so long as the rules are content neutral and are applied in the same manner to all groups wishing to use the space. A library may wish to limit access to exhibit space to groups within the community served by the library. This practice is acceptable provided that the same rules and regulations apply to everyone, and that exclusion is not made on the basis of the doctrinal, religious, or political beliefs of the potential users.

The library should not censor or remove an exhibit because some members of the community may disagree with its content. Those who object to the content of any exhibit held at the library should be able to submit their complaint and/or their own exhibit proposal to be judged according to the policies established by the library.

Libraries may wish to post a permanent notice near the exhibit area stating that the library does not advocate or endorse the viewpoints of exhibits or exhibitors.

Libraries that make bulletin boards available to public groups for posting notices of public interest should develop criteria for the use of these spaces based on the same considerations as those outlined above. Libraries may wish to develop criteria regarding the size of material to be displayed, the length of time materials may remain on the bulletin board, the frequency with which material may be posted for the same group, and the geographic area from which notices will be accepted.

[Adopted July 2, 1991, by the ALA Council; amended June 30, 2004, by the ALA Council]

EXPURGATION OF LIBRARY MATERIALS:
AN INTERPRETATION OF THE LIBRARY BILL OF RIGHTS

Expurgating library materials is a violation of the *Library Bill of Rights*. Expurgation as defined by this interpretation includes any deletion, excision, alteration, editing, or obliteration of any part(s) of books or other library resources by the library, its agent, or its parent institution (if any). By such expurgation, the library is in effect denying access to the complete work and the entire spectrum of ideas that the work intended to express. Such action stands in violation of Articles I, II, and III of the *Library Bill of Rights*, which state that "[m]aterials should not be excluded because of the origin, background, or views of those contributing to their creation," that "[m]aterials should not be proscribed or removed because of partisan or doctrinal disapproval," and that "[l]ibraries should challenge censorship in the fulfillment of their responsibility to provide information and enlightenment."

The act of expurgation has serious implications. It involves a determination that it is necessary to restrict access to the complete work. This is censorship. When a work is expurgated, under the assumption that certain portions of that work would be harmful to minors, the situation is no less serious.

Expurgation of any books or other library resources imposes a restriction, without regard to the rights and desires of all library users, by limiting access to ideas and information.

Further, expurgation without written permission from the holder of the copyright on the material may violate the copyright provisions of the United States Code.

[Adopted February 2, 1973; amended July 1, 1981; amended January 10, 1990, by the ALA Council]

FREE ACCESS TO LIBRARIES FOR MINORS: AN INTERPRETATION OF THE LIBRARY BILL OF RIGHTS

Library policies and procedures that effectively deny minors equal and equitable access to all library resources available to other users violate the *Library Bill of Rights*. The American Library Association opposes all attempts to restrict access to library services, materials, and facilities based on the age of library users.

Article V of the *Library Bill of Rights* states, "A person's right to use a library should not be denied or abridged because of origin, age, background, or views." The "right to use a library" includes free access to, and unrestricted use of, all the services, materials, and facilities the library has to offer. Every restriction on access to, and use of, library resources, based solely on the chronological age, educational level, literacy skills, or legal emancipation of users violates Article V.

Libraries are charged with the mission of developing resources to meet the diverse information needs and interests of the communities they serve. Services, materials, and facilities that fulfill the needs and interests of library users at different stages in their personal development are a necessary part of library resources. The needs and interests of each library user, and resources appropriate to meet those needs and interests, must be determined on an individual basis. Librarians cannot predict what resources will best fulfill the needs and interests of any individual user based on a single criterion such as chronological age, educational level, literacy skills, or legal emancipation.

Libraries should not limit the selection and development of library resources simply because minors will have access to them. Institutional self-censorship diminishes the credibility of the library in the community, and restricts access for all library users.

Children and young adults unquestionably possess *First Amendment* rights, including the right to receive information in the library. Constitutionally protected speech cannot be suppressed solely to protect children or young adults from ideas or images a legislative body believes to be unsuitable for them.[3] Librarians and library governing bodies should not resort to age restrictions in an effort to avoid actual or anticipated objections, because only a court of law can determine whether material is not constitutionally protected.

The mission, goals, and objectives of libraries cannot authorize librarians or library governing bodies to assume, abrogate, or overrule the rights and responsibilities of parents. As "*Libraries: An American Value*" states, "We affirm the responsibility and the right of all parents and guardians to guide their own children's use of the library and its resources and services." Librarians and governing bodies should maintain that parents—and only parents—have the right and the responsibility to restrict the access of their children (and only their children) to library resources. Parents who do not want their children to have access to certain library services, materials, or facilities should so advise their children. Librarians and library governing bodies cannot assume the role of parents or the functions of parental authority in the private relationship between parent and child.

Lack of access to information can be harmful to minors. Librarians and library governing bodies have a public and professional obligation to ensure that all members of the community they serve have free, equal, and equitable access to the entire range of library resources regardless of content, approach, format, or amount of detail. This principle of library service applies equally to all users, minors as well as adults. Librarians and library governing bodies must uphold this principle in order to provide adequate and effective service to minors.

[Adopted June 30, 1972; amended July 1, 1981; July 3, 1991; June 30, 2004, by the ALA Council]

THE FREEDOM TO READ STATEMENT

The freedom to read is essential to our democracy. It is continuously under attack. Private groups and public authorities in various parts of the country are working to remove or limit access to reading materials, to censor content in schools, to label "controversial" views, to distribute lists of "objectionable" books or authors, and to purge libraries. These actions apparently rise from a view that our national tradition of free expression is no longer valid, that censorship and suppression are needed to counter threats to safety or national security, as well as to avoid the subversion of politics and the corruption of morals. We, as individuals devoted to reading and as librarians and publishers responsible for disseminating ideas, wish to assert the public interest in the preservation of the freedom to read.

Most attempts at suppression rest on a denial of the fundamental premise of democracy: that the ordinary individual, by exercising critical judgment, will select the good and reject the bad. We trust Americans to recognize propaganda and misinformation, and to make their own decisions about what they read and believe. We do not believe they are prepared to sacrifice their heritage of a free press in order to be "protected" against what others think may be bad for them. We believe they still favor free enterprise in ideas and expression.

These efforts at suppression are related to a larger pattern of pressures being brought against education, the press, art and images, films, broadcast media, and the Internet. The problem is not only one of actual censorship. The shadow of fear cast by these pressures leads, we suspect, to an even larger voluntary curtailment of expression by those who seek to avoid controversy or unwelcome scrutiny by government officials.

Such pressure toward conformity is perhaps natural to a time of accelerated change. And yet suppression is never more dangerous than in such a time of social tension. Freedom has given the United States the elasticity to endure strain. Freedom keeps open the path of novel and creative solutions, and enables change to come by choice. Every silencing of a heresy, every enforcement of an orthodoxy, diminishes the toughness and resilience of our society and leaves it less able to deal with controversy and difference.

Now, as always in our history, reading is among our greatest freedoms. The freedom to read and write is almost the only means for making generally available ideas or manners of expression that can initially command only a small audience. The written word is the natural medium for the new idea and the untried voice from which come the original contributions to social growth. It is essential to the extended discussion that serious thought requires, and to the accumulation of knowledge and ideas into organized collections.

We believe that free communication is essential to the preservation of a free society and a creative culture. We believe that these pressures toward conformity present the danger of limiting the range and variety of inquiry and expression on which our democracy and our culture depend. We believe that every American community must jealously guard the freedom to publish and to circulate, in order to preserve its own freedom to read. We believe that publishers and librarians have a profound responsibility to give validity to that freedom to read by making it possible for the readers to choose freely from a variety of offerings.

The freedom to read is guaranteed by the Constitution. Those with faith in free people will stand firm on these constitutional guarantees of essential rights and will exercise the responsibilities that accompany these rights.

We therefore affirm these propositions:

1. *It is in the public interest for publishers and librarians to make available the widest diversity of views and expressions, including those that are unorthodox, unpopular, or considered dangerous by the majority.*
   Creative thought is by definition new, and what is new is different. The bearer of every new thought is a rebel until that idea is refined and tested. Totalitarian systems attempt to maintain themselves in power by the ruthless suppression of any concept that challenges the established orthodoxy. The power of a democratic system to adapt to change is vastly strengthened by the freedom of its citizens to choose widely from among conflicting opinions offered freely to them. To stifle every nonconformist idea at birth would mark the end of the democratic process. Furthermore, only through the constant activity of weighing and selecting can the democratic mind attain the strength demanded by times like these. We need to know not only what we believe but why we believe it.

2. *Publishers, librarians, and booksellers do not need to endorse every idea or presentation they make available. It would conflict with the public interest for them to establish their own political, moral, or aesthetic views as a standard for determining what should be published or circulated.*
   Publishers and librarians serve the educational process by helping to make available knowledge and ideas required for the growth of the mind and the increase of learning. They do not foster education by imposing as mentors the patterns of their own thought. The people should have the freedom to read and consider a broader range of ideas than those that may be held by any single librarian or publisher or government or church. It is wrong that what one can read should be confined to what another thinks proper.

3. *It is contrary to the public interest for publishers or librarians to bar access to writings on the basis of the personal history or political affiliations of the author.*
   No art or literature can flourish if it is to be measured by the political views or private lives of its creators. No society of free people can flourish that draws up lists of writers to whom it will not listen, whatever they may have to say.

4. *There is no place in our society for efforts to coerce the taste of others, to confine adults to the reading matter deemed suitable for adolescents, or to inhibit the efforts of writers to achieve artistic expression.*

   To some, much of modern expression is shocking. But is not much of life itself shocking? We cut off literature at the source if we prevent writers from dealing with the stuff of life. Parents and teachers have a responsibility to prepare the young to meet the diversity of experiences in life to which they will be exposed, as they have a responsibility to help them learn to think critically for themselves. These are affirmative responsibilities, not to be discharged simply by preventing them from reading works for which they are not yet prepared. In these matters values differ, and values cannot be legislated, nor can machinery be devised that will suit the demands of one group without limiting the freedom of others.

5. *It is not in the public interest to force a reader to accept the prejudgment of a label characterizing any expression or its author as subversive or dangerous.*

   The ideal of labeling presupposes the existence of individuals or groups with wisdom to determine by authority what is good or bad for others. It presupposes that individuals must be directed in making up their minds about the ideas they examine. But Americans do not need others to do their thinking for them.

6. *It is the responsibility of publishers and librarians, as guardians of the people's freedom to read, to contest encroachments upon that freedom by individuals or groups seeking to impose their own standards or tastes upon the community at large and by the government whenever it seeks to reduce or deny public access to public information.*

   It is inevitable in the give and take of the democratic process that the political, the moral, or the aesthetic concepts of an individual or group will occasionally collide with those of another individual or group. In a free society individuals are free to determine for themselves what they wish to read, and each group is free to determine what it will recommend to its freely associated members. But no group has the right to take the law into its own hands and to impose its own concept of politics or morality upon other members of a democratic society. Freedom is no freedom if it is accorded only to the accepted and the inoffensive. Further, democratic societies are more safe, free, and creative when the free flow of public information is not restricted by governmental prerogative or self-censorship.

7. *It is the responsibility of publishers and librarians to give full meaning to the freedom to read by providing books that enrich the quality and diversity of thought and expression. By the exercise of this affirmative*

responsibility, they can demonstrate that the answer to a "bad" book is a good one, the answer to a "bad" idea is a good one.

The freedom to read is of little consequence when the reader cannot obtain matter fit for that reader's purpose. What is needed is not only the absence of restraint, but the positive provision of opportunity for the people to read the best that has been thought and said. Books are the major channel by which the intellectual inheritance is handed down, and the principal means of its testing and growth. The defense of the freedom to read requires of all publishers and librarians the utmost of their faculties, and deserves of all Americans the fullest of their support.

We state these propositions neither lightly nor as easy generalizations. We here stake out a lofty claim for the value of the written word. We do so because we believe that it is possessed of enormous variety and usefulness, worthy of cherishing and keeping free. We realize that the application of these propositions may mean the dissemination of ideas and manners of expression that are repugnant to many persons. We do not state these propositions in the comfortable belief that what people read is unimportant. We believe rather that what people read is deeply important, that ideas can be dangerous, but that the suppression of ideas is fatal to a democratic society. Freedom itself is a dangerous way of life, but it is ours.

This statement was originally issued in May of 1953 by the Westchester Conference of the American Library Association and the American Book Publishers Council, which in 1970 consolidated with the American Educational Publishers Institute to become the Association of American Publishers. [Adopted June 25, 1953; revised January 28, 1972; January 16, 1991; July 12, 2000; June 30, 2004, by the ALA Council and the AAP Freedom to Read Committee]

THE FREEDOM TO VIEW STATEMENT

The freedom to view, along with the freedom to speak, to hear, and to read, is protected by the *First Amendment to the Constitution of the United States*. In a free society, there is no place for censorship of any medium of expression. Therefore these principles are affirmed:

1. To provide the broadest access to film, video, and other audiovisual materials because they are a means for the communication of ideas. Liberty of circulation is essential to insure the constitutional guarantees of freedom of expression.

2. To protect the confidentiality of all individuals and institutions using film, video, and other audiovisual materials.
3. To provide film, video, and other audiovisual materials which represent a diversity of views and expression. Selection of a work does not constitute or imply agreement with or approval of the content.
4. To provide a diversity of viewpoints without the constraint of labeling or prejudging film, video, or other audiovisual materials on the basis of the moral, religious, or political beliefs of the producer or filmmaker or on the basis of controversial content.
5. To contest vigorously, by all lawful means, every encroachment upon the public's freedom to view.

This statement was originally drafted by the Freedom to View Committee of the American Film and Video Association (formerly the Educational Film Library Association) and was adopted by the AFVA Board of Directors in February 1979. This statement was updated and approved by the AFVA Board of Directors in 1989.
[Endorsed by the ALA Council January 10, 1990]

GUIDELINES FOR THE DEVELOPMENT AND IMPLEMENTATION OF POLICIES, REGULATIONS AND PROCEDURES AFFECTING ACCESS TO LIBRARY MATERIALS, SERVICES AND FACILITIES

Publicly supported libraries exist within the context of a body of law derived from the United States Constitution and appropriate state constitutions, defined by statute, and implemented by regulations, policies and procedures established by their governing bodies and administrations. These regulations, policies and procedures establish the mission of the library, define its functions, services and operations and ascertain the rights and responsibilities of the clientele served by the library.

Publicly supported library service is based upon the *First Amendment* right of free expression. The publicly supported library provides free and equal access to information for all people of the community it serves. Thus, publicly supported libraries are governmental agencies designated as limited public forums for access to information. Libraries that make meeting rooms, exhibit spaces and/or bulletin boards available for public use are also designated as limited public forums for the exchange of information.

Many libraries adopt administrative policies and procedures regulating the organization and use of library materials, services and facilities. These policies and procedures affect access and may have the effect of restricting, denying or creating barriers to access to the library as a public forum, including the library's resources, facilities and services. Library policies and procedures that impinge upon *First Amendment* rights are subject to a higher standard of review than may be required in the policies of other public services and facilities.

Policies, procedures or regulations that may result in denying, restricting or creating physical or economic barriers to access to the library's public forum must be based on a compelling government interest. However, library governing authorities may place reasonable and narrowly drawn restrictions on the time, place or manner of access to library resources, services or facilities, provided that such restrictions are not based upon arbitrary distinctions between individuals or classes of individuals.

The American Library Association has adopted the *Library Bill of Rights* and *Interpretations of the Library Bill of Rights* to provide library governing authorities, librarians and other library staff and library users with guidelines on how constitutional principles apply to libraries in the United States of America.

The American Library Association's Intellectual Freedom Committee recommends that publicly supported libraries use the following guidelines, based on constitutional principles, to develop policies, regulations and procedures.

Guidelines

All library policies, regulations and procedures should be carefully examined to determine if they may result in denying, restricting or creating barriers to access. If they may result in such restrictions, they

1. should be developed and implemented within the legal framework that applies to the library. This includes the *United States Constitution*, including the First and Fourteenth Amendments, due process and equal treatment under the law; the applicable state constitution; federal and state civil rights legislation; all other applicable federal, state and local legislation; and applicable case law;
2. should cite statutes or ordinances upon which the authority to make that policy is based, when appropriate;
3. should be developed and implemented within the framework of the *Library Bill of Rights* and its Interpretations;
4. should be based upon the library's mission and objectives;
5. should only impose restrictions on the access to, or use of library resources, services or facilities when those restrictions are necessary to achieve the library's mission and objectives;

6. should narrowly tailor prohibitions or restrictions, in the rare instances when they are required, so they are not more restrictive than needed to serve their objectives;

7. should attempt to balance competing interests and avoid favoring the majority at the expense of individual rights, or allowing individual users' rights to interfere materially with the majority's rights to free and equal access to library resources, services and facilities;

8. should avoid arbitrary distinctions between individuals or classes of users, and should not have the effect of denying or abridging a person's right to use library resources, services or facilities based upon arbitrary distinctions such as origin, age, background or views. In the *Library Bill of Rights* and all of its Interpretations, it is intended that: "origin" encompasses all the characteristics of individuals that are inherent in the circumstances of their birth, "age" encompasses all the characteristics of individuals that are inherent in their levels of development and maturity, "background" encompasses all the characteristics of individuals that are a result of their life experiences, and "views" encompasses all the opinions and beliefs held and expressed by individuals;

9. should not target specific users or groups of users based upon an assumption or expectation that such users might engage in behavior that will materially interfere with the achievement of substantial library objectives;

10. must be clearly stated so that a reasonably intelligent person will have fair warning of what is expected;

11. must provide a means of appeal;

12. must be reviewed regularly by the library's governing authority and by its legal counsel;

13. must be communicated clearly and made available in an effective manner to all library users;

14. must be enforced evenhandedly and not in a manner intended to benefit or disfavor any person or group in an arbitrary or capricious manner. Libraries should develop an ongoing staff training program designed to foster the understanding of the legal framework and principles underlying library policies and to assist staff in gaining the skill and ability to respond to potentially difficult circumstances in a timely, direct and open manner. This program should include training to develop empathy and understanding of the social and economic problems of some library users;

15. should, if reasonably possible, provide adequate alternative means of access to information for those whose behavior results in the denial or restriction of access to any library resource, service or facility.

[Adopted by the ALA Intellectual Freedom Committee June 28, 1994]

GUIDELINES FOR THE DEVELOPMENT OF POLICIES AND PROCEDURES REGARDING USER BEHAVIOR AND LIBRARY USAGE

Libraries are faced with problems of user behavior that must be addressed to insure the effective delivery of service and full access to facilities. Library governing bodies must approach the regulation of user behavior within the framework of the *ALA Code of Ethics*, the *Library Bill of Rights* and the law, including local and state statutes, constitutional standards under the First and Fourteenth Amendments, due process, and equal treatment under the law.

Publicly supported library service is based upon the *First Amendment* right of free expression. Publicly supported libraries are recognized as limited public forums for access to information. At least one federal court of appeals has recognized a *First Amendment* right to receive information in a public library. Library policies and procedures that could impinge upon such rights are subject to a higher standard of review than may be required in the policies of other public services and facilities.

There is a significant government interest in maintaining a library environment that is conducive to all users' exercise of their constitutionally protected right to receive information. This significant interest authorizes publicly supported libraries to maintain a safe and healthy environment in which library users and staff can be free from harassment, intimidation, and threats to their safety and well-being. Libraries should provide appropriate safeguards against such behavior and enforce policies and procedures addressing that behavior when it occurs.

In order to protect all library users' right of access to library facilities, to ensure the safety of users and staff, and to protect library resources and facilities from damage, the library's governing authority may impose reasonable restrictions on the time, place, or manner of library access.

Guidelines

The American Library Association's Intellectual Freedom Committee recommends that publicly supported libraries use the following guidelines, based upon constitutional principles, to develop policies and procedures governing the use of library facilities:

1. Libraries are advised to rely upon existing legislation and law enforcement mechanisms as the primary means of controlling behavior that involves public safety, criminal behavior, or other issues covered by exist-

ing local, state, or federal statutes. In many instances, this legal framework may be sufficient to provide the library with the necessary tools to maintain order.

2. If the library's governing body chooses to write its own policies and procedures regarding user behavior or access to library facilities, services, and resources, the policies should cite statutes or ordinances upon which the authority to make those policies is based.

3. Library policies and procedures governing the use of library facilities should be carefully examined to insure that they are not in violation of the *Library Bill of Rights*.

4. Reasonable and narrowly drawn policies and procedures designed to prohibit interference with use of the facilities and services by others, or to prohibit activities inconsistent with achievement of the library's mission statement and objectives, are acceptable.

5. Such policies and the attendant implementing procedures should be reviewed frequently and updated as needed by the library's legal counsel for compliance with federal and state constitutional requirements, federal and state civil rights legislation, all other applicable federal and state legislation, and applicable case law.

6. Every effort should be made to respond to potentially difficult circumstances of user behavior in a timely, direct, and open manner. Common sense, reason and sensitivity should be used to resolve issues in a constructive and positive manner without escalation.

7. Libraries should develop an ongoing staff training program based upon their user behavior policy. This program should include training to develop empathy and understanding of the social and economic problems of some library users.

8. Policies and regulations that impose restrictions on library access

   a. should apply only to those activities that materially interfere with the public's right of access to library facilities, the safety of users and staff, and the protection of library resources and facilities;

   b. should narrowly tailor prohibitions or restrictions so that they are not more restrictive than needed to serve their objectives;

   c. should attempt to balance competing interests and avoid favoring the majority at the expense of individual rights, or allowing individual users' rights to supersede those of the majority of library users;

   d. should be based solely upon actual behavior and not upon arbitrary distinctions between individuals or classes of individuals. Policies should not target specific users or groups of users based upon an assumption or expectation that such users might engage in behaviors that could disrupt library service;

e. should not restrict access to the library by persons who merely inspire the anger or annoyance of others. Policies based upon appearance or behavior that is merely annoying or which merely generates negative subjective reactions from others, do not meet the necessary standard. Such policies should employ a reasonable, objective standard based on the behavior itself;

f. must provide a clear description of the behavior that is prohibited and the various enforcement measures in place so that a reasonably intelligent person will have both due process and fair warning; this description must be continuously and clearly communicated in an effective manner to all library users;

g. to the extent possible, should not leave those affected without adequate alternative means of access to information in the library; and

h. must be enforced evenhandedly, and not in a manner intended to benefit or disfavor any person or group in an arbitrary or capricious manner.

The user behaviors addressed in these Guidelines are the result of a wide variety of individual and societal conditions. Libraries should take advantage of the expertise of local social service agencies, advocacy groups, mental health professionals, law enforcement officials, and other community resources to develop community strategies for addressing the needs of a diverse population.

[Adopted by the Intellectual Freedom Committee January 24, 1993; revised November 17, 2000]

LIBRARY BILL OF RIGHTS

The American Library Association affirms that all libraries are forums for information and ideas and that the following basic policies should guide their services.

I. Books and other library resources should be provided for the interest, information, and enlightenment of all people of the community the library serves. Materials should not be excluded because of the origin, background, or views of those contributing to their creation.

II. Libraries should provide materials and information presenting all points of view on current and historical issues. Materials should not be proscribed or removed because of partisan or doctrinal disapproval.

III. Libraries should challenge censorship in the fulfillment of their responsibility to provide information and enlightenment.

IV. Libraries should cooperate with all persons and groups concerned with resisting abridgment of free expression and free access to ideas.
V. A person's right to use a library should not be denied or abridged because of origin, age, background, or views.
VI. Libraries which make exhibit spaces and meeting rooms available to the public they serve should make such facilities available on an equitable basis, regardless of the beliefs or affiliations of individuals or groups requesting their use.

[Adopted June 18, 1948. Amended February 2, 1961, and January 23, 1980, inclusion of "age" reaffirmed January 23, 1996, by the ALA Council]

LIBRARY-INITIATED PROGRAMS AS A RESOURCE: AN INTERPRETATION OF THE LIBRARY BILL OF RIGHTS

Library-initiated programs support the mission of the library by providing users with additional opportunities for information, education, and recreation. Article I of the *Library Bill of Rights* states, "Books and other library resources should be provided for the interest, information, and enlightenment of all people of the community the library serves."

Library-initiated programs take advantage of library staff expertise, collections, services, and facilities to increase access to information and information resources. Library-initiated programs introduce users and potential users to the resources of the library and to the library's primary function as a facilitator of information access. The library may participate in cooperative or joint programs with other agencies, organizations, institutions, or individuals as part of its own effort to address information needs and to facilitate information access in the community the library serves.

Library-initiated programs on-site and in other locations include, but are not limited to, speeches, community forums, discussion groups, demonstrations, displays, and live or media presentations.

Libraries serving multilingual or multicultural communities should make efforts to accommodate the information needs of those for whom English is a second language. Library-initiated programs that cross language and cultural barriers introduce otherwise underserved populations to the resources of the library and provide access to information.

Library-initiated programs "should not be proscribed or removed [or canceled] because of partisan or doctrinal disapproval" of the contents of the program or the views expressed by the participants, as stated in Article II of the *Library Bill of Rights*. Library sponsorship of a program does not constitute an endorsement of the content of the program or the views expressed by the participants, any more than the purchase of material for the library collection constitutes an endorsement of the contents of the material or the views of its creator.

Library-initiated programs are a library resource, and, as such, are developed in accordance with written guidelines, as approved and adopted by the library's policy-making body. These guidelines should include an endorsement of the *Library Bill of Rights* and set forth the library's commitment to free and open access to information and ideas for all users.

Library staff select topics, speakers and resource materials for library-initiated programs based on the interests and information needs of the community. Topics, speakers, and resource materials are not excluded from library-initiated programs because of possible controversy. Concerns, questions, or complaints about library-initiated programs are handled according to the same written policy and procedures that govern reconsiderations of other library resources.

Library-initiated programs are offered free of charge and are open to all. Article V of the *Library Bill of Rights* states, "A person's right to use a library should not be denied or abridged because of origin, age, background, or views."

The "right to use a library" encompasses all the resources the library offers, including the right to attend library-initiated programs. Libraries do not deny or abridge access to library resources, including library-initiated programs, based on an individual's economic background or ability to pay.

[Adopted January 27, 1982; amended June 26, 1990; July 12, 2000, by the ALA Council]

POLICY CONCERNING CONFIDENTIALITY OF PERSONALLY IDENTIFIABLE INFORMATION ABOUT LIBRARY USERS

"In a library (physical or virtual), the right to privacy is the right to open inquiry without having the subject of one's interest examined or scrutinized by others. Confidentiality exists when a library is in possession of personally identifiable information about users and keeps that information private on their behalf" (*Privacy: An Interpretation of the Library Bill of Rights*).

The ethical responsibilities of librarians, as well as statutes in most states and the District of Columbia, protect the privacy of library users. Confidentiality extends to "information sought or received and resources consulted, borrowed, acquired or transmitted" (*ALA Code of Ethics*), and includes, but is not limited to, database search records, reference interviews, circulation records, interlibrary loan records, and other personally identifiable uses of library materials, facilities, or services.

The First Amendment's guarantee of freedom of speech and of the press requires that the corresponding rights to hear what is spoken and read what is written be preserved, free from fear of government intrusion, intimidation, or reprisal. The American Library Association reaffirms its opposition to "any use of governmental prerogatives that lead to the intimidation of individuals or groups and discourages them from exercising the right of free expression as guaranteed by the First Amendment to the U.S. Constitution" and "encourages resistance to such abuse of governmental power" (*ALA Policy 53.4*). In seeking access or in the pursuit of information, confidentiality is the primary means of providing the privacy that will free the individual from fear of intimidation or retaliation.

The American Library Association regularly receives reports of visits by agents of federal, state, and local law enforcement agencies to libraries, asking for personally identifiable information about library users. These visits, whether under the rubric of simply informing libraries of agency concerns or for some other reason, reflect an insensitivity to the legal and ethical bases for confidentiality, and the role it plays in the preservation of *First Amendment* rights, rights also extended to foreign nationals while in the United States. The government's interest in library use reflects a dangerous and fallacious equation of what a person reads with what that person believes or how that person is likely to behave. Such a presumption can and does threaten the freedom of access to information. It also is a threat to a crucial aspect of First Amendment rights: that freedom of speech and of the press include the freedom to hold, disseminate, and receive unpopular, minority, extreme, or even dangerous ideas.

The American Library Association recognizes that law enforcement agencies and officers may occasionally believe that library records contain information that would be helpful to the investigation of criminal activity. The American judicial system provides the mechanism for seeking release of such confidential records: a court order, following a showing of *good cause* based on *specific facts*, by a court of competent jurisdiction.[4]

The American Library Association also recognizes that, under limited circumstances, access to certain information might be restricted due to a legitimate national security concern. However, there has been no showing of a plausible probability that national security will be compromised by any use made of unclassified information available in libraries. Access to this unclassified information should be handled no differently than access to any other information. Therefore, libraries and librarians have a legal and ethical responsibility to protect the confidentiality of all library users, including foreign nationals.

Libraries are one of the great bulwarks of democracy. They are living embodiments of the First Amendment because their collections include voices of

dissent as well as assent. Libraries are impartial resources providing information on all points of view, available to all persons regardless of origin, age, background, or views. The role of libraries as such a resource must not be compromised by an erosion of the privacy rights of library users.
[Adopted July 2, 1991; amended June 30, 2004, by the ALA Council]

POLICY ON GOVERNMENTAL INTIMIDATION

The American Library Association opposes any use of governmental prerogatives that lead to the intimidation of individuals or groups and discourages them from exercising the right of free expression as guaranteed by the *First Amendment* to the US Constitution. ALA encourages resistance to such abuse of governmental power and supports those against whom such governmental power has been employed.
[Adopted February 2, 1973; amended July 1, 1981; June 30, 2004, by the ALA Council]

REGULATIONS, POLICIES, AND PROCEDURES AFFECTING ACCESS TO LIBRARY RESOURCES AND SERVICES

The reconsideration form is instrumental in determining whether materials under fire are to be retained in the library collection.

REQUEST FOR RECONSIDERATION OF LIBRARY RESOURCES

IMPORTANT: The entire form must be completed in order for an item to be reconsidered.

PLEASE PRINT

Date: _____

Request initiated by: _____

Address: _____ Telephone: _____

Complainant represents:

_____ him/herself

_____ organization: _____

FORMAT: ___ Book ___ Video ___ Audio cassette ___ Compact disc ___

Book-on-Tape ____ other (specify) _____

Author/Artist/Director: _____

Title: _____

Publisher/Producer: _____

1. Did you read/view/listen to the entire item? _____
Parts _____
2. To what do you object: (Cite pages, scenes, etc.) _____
_____
_____

3. To what do you approve: (Cite pages, scenes, etc.) _____
_____
_____

4. What do you believe is the theme of this book/video/audio recording? __
_____
_____

5. What do you feel might be the result of reading/viewing/hearing this material? _____
_____

6. Are you aware of the judgment of this material by critics? _____
_____

7. What would you like the library to do about this item? _____
_____
_____

8. What alternative book/video/audio recording of equal quality do you recommend that will convey a similar perspective? _____
_____
_____

Signature _____

RESOLUTION ON ACCESS TO THE USE OF LIBRARIES AND INFORMATION BY INDIVIDUALS WITH PHYSICAL OR MENTAL IMPAIRMENT

Whereas, The Intellectual Freedom Committee is concerned with freedom of access; and

Whereas, The *Library Bill of Rights* states that "books and other library resources should be provided for the interests, information, and enlightenment of all people of the community the library serves" and "a person's right to use a library should not be denied or abridged"; and

Whereas, Federal and state constitutional and statutory laws forbid public institutions from discriminating against handicapped individuals, i.e., persons who have a physical or mental impairment; and

Whereas, Court opinions have clearly interpreted said laws as proscribing discrimination against persons who have acquired immune deficiency syndrome ("AIDS"), AIDS-related complex ("ARC"), or who test positive for the human immunodeficiency virus ("HIV"); and

Whereas, The American Medical Association and the United States Department of Health and Human Services have opined that while the human immunodeficiency virus that causes AIDS is a contagious disease, it cannot be transmitted by casual contact; now, therefore be it

Resolved, That the *Library Bill of Rights* of the American Library Association which insures access to library facilities, materials and services by all people of the community includes individuals with physical or mental impairments; and be it further

Resolved, That the American Library Association deplores discrimination against and denial or abridgment of library and information access to persons of all ages who have acquired immune deficiency syndrome ("AIDS"), AIDS-related complex ("ARC"), or who test positive for the human immunodeficiency virus ("HIV").

[Adopted January 13, 1988, by the ALA Council]

RESOLUTION ON THE USE OF
FILTERING SOFTWARE IN LIBRARIES

WHEREAS, On June 26, 1997, the United States Supreme Court issued a *sweeping re-affirmation of core First Amendment principles* and held that communications over the Internet deserve the highest level of Constitutional protection; and

WHEREAS, The Court's most fundamental holding is that communications on the Internet deserve the same level of Constitutional protection as books, magazines, newspapers, and speakers on a street corner soapbox. The Court found that the Internet "constitutes a vast platform from which to address and hear from a world-wide audience of millions of readers, viewers, researchers, and buyers," and that "any person with a phone line can become a town crier with a voice that resonates farther than it could from any soapbox"; and

WHEREAS, For libraries, the most critical holding of the Supreme Court is that libraries that make content available on the Internet can continue to do so with the same Constitutional protections that apply to the books on libraries' shelves; and

WHEREAS, The Court's conclusion that "the vast democratic fora of the Internet" merit full constitutional protection will also serve to protect libraries that provide their patrons with access to the Internet; and

WHEREAS, The Court recognized the importance of enabling individuals to receive speech from the entire world and to speak to the entire world. Libraries provide those opportunities to many who would not otherwise have them; and

WHEREAS, The Supreme Court's decision will protect that access; and

WHEREAS, The use in libraries of software filters which block Constitutionally protected speech is inconsistent with the United States Constitution and federal law and may lead to legal exposure for the library and its governing authorities; now, therefore, be it

RESOLVED, That the American Library Association affirms that the use of filtering software by libraries to block access to constitutionally protected speech violates the *Library Bill of Rights*.

[Adopted by the ALA Council, July 2, 1997]

RESTRICTED ACCESS TO LIBRARY MATERIALS:
AN INTERPRETATION OF THE LIBRARY BILL OF RIGHTS

Libraries are a traditional forum for the open exchange of information. Attempts to restrict access to library materials violate the basic tenets of the *Library Bill of Rights*.

Some libraries place materials in a "closed shelf," "locked case," "adults only," "restricted shelf," or "high-demand" collection. Some libraries have applied filtering software to their Internet stations to prevent users from finding targeted categories of information, much of which is constitutionally protected. Some libraries block access to certain materials by placing other barriers between the user and those materials.

Because restricted materials often deal with controversial, unusual, or sensitive subjects, having to ask a librarian or circulation clerk for access to them may be embarrassing or inhibiting for patrons desiring the materials. Requiring a user to ask for materials may create a service barrier or pose a language-skills barrier. Even when a title is listed in the catalog with a reference to its restricted status, a barrier is placed between the patron and the publication.[5] Because restricted materials often feature information that some people consider objectionable, potential library users may be predisposed to think of the materials as objectionable and, therefore, be reluctant to ask for access to them.

Limiting access by relegating materials into physically or virtually restricted or segregated collections or restricting materials by creating age-related, linguistic, economic, psychological, or other barriers violates the Library Bill of Rights. However, some libraries have established restrictive policies to protect their materials from theft or mutilation, or because of statutory authority or institutional mandate. Such policies must be carefully formulated and administered to ensure they do not violate established principles of intellectual freedom. This caution is reflected in ALA policies, such as *Evaluating Library Collections*, *Free Access to Libraries for Minors*, *Preservation Policy*, and the ACRL *Code of Ethics for Special Collections Librarians*.

In keeping with the *Joint Statement on Access* of the American Library Association and Society of American Archivists, libraries should avoid accepting donor agreements or entering into contracts that impose permanent restrictions on special collections. As stated in the "Joint Statement," it is the responsibility of libraries with such collections "to make available original research materials in its possession on equal terms of access."

All proposals for restricted access collections should be carefully scrutinized to ensure that the purpose is not to suppress a viewpoint or to place a barrier between certain patrons and particular content. A primary goal of the library profession is to facilitate access to all points of view on current and historical issues.

[Adopted February 2, 1973; amended July 1, 1981; July 3, 1991; July 12, 2000; June 30, 2004, by the ALA Council]

STATEMENT ON LABELING:
AN INTERPRETATION OF THE LIBRARY BILL OF RIGHTS

Labeling is the practice of describing or designating materials by affixing a prejudicial label and/or segregating them by a prejudicial system. The American Library Association opposes these means of predisposing people's attitudes toward library materials for the following reasons:

1. Labeling is an attempt to prejudice attitudes and as such, it is a censor's tool.
2. Some find it easy and even proper, according to their ethics, to establish criteria for judging publications as objectionable. However, injustice and ignorance rather than justice and enlightenment result from such practices, and the American Library Association opposes the establishment of such criteria.
3. Libraries do not advocate the ideas found in their collections. The presence of books and other resources in a library does not indicate endorsement of their contents by the library.

A variety of private organizations promulgate rating systems and/or review materials as a means of advising either their members or the general public concerning their opinions of the contents and suitability or appropriate age for use of certain books, films, recordings, or other materials. For the library to adopt or enforce any of these private systems, to attach such ratings to library materials, to include them in bibliographic records, library catalogs, or other finding aids, or otherwise to endorse them would violate the *Library Bill of Rights*.

While some attempts have been made to adopt these systems into law, the constitutionality of such measures is extremely questionable. If such legislation is passed which applies within a library's jurisdiction, the library should seek competent legal advice concerning its applicability to library operations.

Publishers, industry groups, and distributors sometimes add ratings to material or include them as part of their packaging. Librarians should not endorse such practices. However, removing or obliterating such ratings—if placed there by or with permission of the copyright holder—could constitute expurgation, which is also unacceptable.

The American Library Association opposes efforts which aim at closing any path to knowledge. This statement, however, does not exclude the adoption of organizational schemes designed as directional aids or to facilitate access to materials.

[Adopted July 13, 1951. Amended June 25, 1971; July 1, 1981; June 26, 1990, by the ALA Council]

THE UNIVERSAL RIGHT TO FREE EXPRESSION: AN INTERPRETATION OF THE LIBRARY BILL OF RIGHTS

Freedom of expression is an inalienable human right and the foundation for self-government. Freedom of expression encompasses the freedoms of speech, press, religion, assembly, and association, and the corollary right to receive information.

The American Library Association endorses this principle, which is also set forth in the *Universal Declaration of Human Rights*, adopted by the United Nations General Assembly. The Preamble of this document states that "recognition of the inherent dignity and of the equal and inalienable rights of all members of the human family is the foundation of freedom, justice, and peace in the world" and "the advent of a world in which human beings shall enjoy freedom of speech and belief and freedom from fear and want has been proclaimed as the highest aspiration of the common people."

Article 18 of this document states,

Everyone has the right to freedom of thought, conscience, and religion; this right includes freedom to change his religion or belief, and freedom, either alone or in community with others and in public or private, to manifest his religion or belief in teaching, practice, worship, and observance.

Article 19 states,

Everyone has the right to freedom of opinion and expression; this right includes freedom to hold opinions without interference and to seek, receive, and impart information and ideas through any media regardless of frontiers.

Article 20 states,

1. Everyone has the right to freedom of peaceful assembly and association.
2. No one may be compelled to belong to an association.

We affirm our belief that these are inalienable rights of every person, regardless of origin, age, background, or views. We embody our professional commitment to these principles in the *Library Bill of Rights* and *Code of Ethics*, as adopted by the American Library Association.

We maintain that these are universal principles and should be applied by libraries and librarians throughout the world. The American Library Association's policy on International Relations reflects these objectives: "to encourage the exchange, dissemination, and access to information and the unrestricted flow of library materials in all formats throughout the world."

We know that censorship, ignorance, and limitations on the free flow of information are the tools of tyranny and oppression. We believe that ideas and information topple the walls of hate and fear and build bridges of cooperation and understanding far more effectively than weapons and armies.

The American Library Association is unswerving in its commitment to human rights and intellectual freedom; the two are inseparably linked and inextricably entwined. Freedom of opinion and expression is not derived from or dependent on any form of government or political power. This right is inherent in every individual. It cannot be surrendered, nor can it be denied. True justice comes from the exercise of this right.

We recognize the power of information and ideas to inspire justice, to restore freedom and dignity to the oppressed, and to change the hearts and minds of the oppressors.

Courageous men and women, in difficult and dangerous circumstances throughout human history, have demonstrated that freedom lives in the human heart and cries out for justice even in the face of threats, enslavement, imprisonment, torture, exile, and death. We draw inspiration from their example. They challenge us to remain steadfast in our most basic professional responsibility to promote and defend the right of free expression.

There is no good censorship. Any effort to restrict free expression and the free flow of information aids the oppressor. Fighting oppression with censorship is self-defeating.

Threats to the freedom of expression of any person anywhere are threats to the freedom of all people everywhere. Violations of human rights and the right of free expression have been recorded in virtually every country and society across the globe.

In response to these violations, we affirm these principles:

- The American Library Association opposes any use of *governmental prerogative* that leads to the intimidation of individuals that prevents them from exercising their rights to hold opinions without interference, and to seek, receive, and impart information and ideas. We urge libraries and librarians everywhere to resist such abuse of governmental power, and to support those against whom such governmental power has been employed.
- The American Library Association condemns any governmental effort to involve libraries and librarians in restrictions on the right of any individual to hold opinions without interference, and to seek, receive, and impart information and ideas. Such restrictions pervert the function of the library and violate the professional responsibilities of librarians.
- The American Library Association rejects censorship in any form. Any action that denies the inalienable human rights of individuals only damages the will to resist oppression, strengthens the hand of the oppressor, and undermines the cause of justice.
- The American Library Association will not abrogate these principles. We believe that censorship corrupts the cause of justice, and contributes to the demise of freedom.

[Adopted by the ALA Council, January 16, 1991]

NOTES

1. See *Free Access to Libraries for Minors: An Interpretation of the Library Bill of Rights; Access to Resources and Services in the School Library Media Program: An Interpretation of the Library Bill of Rights;* and *Access for Children and Young People to Videotapes and Other Nonprint Formats: An Interpretation of the Library Bill of Rights.*

2. See *Diversity in Collection Development: An Interpretation of the Library Bill of Rights.*

3. See *Erznoznik v. City of Jacksonville,* 422 U.S. 205 (1975)—"Speech that is neither obscene as to youths nor subject to some other legitimate proscription cannot be

suppressed solely to protect the young from ideas or images that a legislative body thinks unsuitable [422 U.S. 205, 214] for them. In most circumstances, the values protected by the First Amendment are no less applicable when government seeks to control the flow of information to minors. *See Tinker v. Des Moines School Dist., supra. Cf. West Virginia Bd. of Ed. v. Barnette*, 319 U.S. 624 (1943)."

4. See *Confidentiality and Coping with Law Enforcement Inquiries: Guidelines for the Library and Its Staff*, ALA Office for Intellectual Freedom, available on the Web at www.ala.org/oif/ifissues.

5. See also *Statement on Labeling*.

Index

About the Authors

Dr. Frank W. Hoffmann is a professor of library science at Sam Houston State University in Huntsville, Texas. He teaches courses relating to information services, collection development, research methods, and popular music. He received his BA (1971) and MLS (1972) from Indiana University, Bloomington, and his PhD (1977) from the University of Pittsburgh. He has written more than thirty-five books devoted to music, collection development, intellectual freedom, fads, and popular culture. A lifelong record collector, he has been utilized as a subject expert by A&E Television, the History Channel, the *New York Times*, and many other news publications. His articles have appeared in numerous encyclopedias and journals, including the *Encyclopedia of Recorded Sound*, *International Music Journals*, the *Encyclopedia of Library and Information Science*, *Magazines for Libraries*, *Urtich's Guide to Periodicals*, *Cash Box*, *Popular Music and Society*, *School Library Journal*, *Popular Culture in Libraries*, and *Victrola and 78 Journal*.

Dr. Richard Wood is dean of the University of South Alabama Library System. He previously has served as the director of the Citadel Library and Sam Houston State University's Newton Gresham Library. He received his MLS and PhD in Library Science from the University of Pittsburgh. He has written a dozen books and numerous professional articles on library collection management and other scholarly issues.